Prose & Life Writing

egg box

UEA Creative Writing Anthology 2012

First published by Egg Box Publishing 2012
International © retained by individual authors

This book is sold subject to the condition that it shall not, by way of trade or otherwise, be lent, resold, hired out, stored in a retrieval system, or otherwise circulated without the publisher's prior consent in any form of binding or cover other than that in which it is published and without a similar condition including this condition being imposed on the subsequent purchaser.

A CIP record for this book is available from the British Library.

UEA Creative Writing Anthology 2012 is typeset in Caslon 10pt on 13pt leading with Din titles.

Printed and bound in the UK by CPI Antony Rowe Ltd.

Designed and typeset by Sean Purdy at The Ampersand.

Cover photography by Wil Abbott-Howes.

Proofread by Sarah Gooderson.

Distributed by Central Books.
ISBN: 9780956928931

Acknowledgments

Thanks to the following for making this anthology possible:

The Malcolm Bradbury Memorial Fund, the Centre for Creative and Performing Arts at the University of East Anglia and The School of Literature, Drama and Creative Writing at UEA in partnership with Egg Box Publishing.

We'd also like to thank the following people:

Moniza Alvi, Jean Boase-Beier, Amit Chaudhuri, Andrew Cowan, William Fiennes, Giles Foden, Sarah Gooderson, Lavinia Greenlaw, Rachel Hore, Kathryn Hughes, Katie Konyn, Michael Lengsfield, Jean McNeil, Natalie Mitchell, Jeremy Page, Rob Ritchie, Helen Smith, Henry Sutton, George Szirtes, Val Taylor and Steve Waters.

Nathan Hamilton at Egg Box Publishing, Sean Purdy at The Ampersand and Wil Abbot-Howes.

Editorial team:
Linda Black
Natasha Broad
Gaynor Clements
Ella Chappell
Eluned Gramich
Tilly Lunken
Erin Meier
Judy O'Kane

Contents

Foreword
Andrew Miller — *I*

Prose Introduction
Henry Sutton — *10*

Contributors
Joshua Bruce Allen — *14*
Gaynor Clements — *20*
Jack Davidson — *26*
Tom Raphael Eaves — *32*
Eluned Gramich — *38*
Jessica Granatt — *44*
Rebecca Tyng Kantor — *52*
Kate Macrae — *58*
Peter Matthews — *64*
Erin Meier — *70*
Anna Metcalfe — *74*
Will Miles — *78*
Claire Powell — *86*
Natasha Pulley — *92*
Eliza Robertson — *98*

Sara Sha'ath	–	*104*
Kim Sherwood	–	*110*
Dennison Smith	–	*116*
Siobhan Tumelty	–	*122*
Fuchsia Wilkins	–	*128*

Life Writing Introduction
Kathryn Hughes — *136*

Contributors
Judith Chriqui	–	*138*
Judy O'Kane	–	*140*
Stephen Skelton	–	*146*
Adrian Ward	–	*155*

Foreword

by Andrew Miller

There were nine of us, including a Canadian, an Irishman and an Icelander. The group 'father' was the lovable John Wakeham, already an experienced editor and publisher of poetry. The rest of us were between twenty-five and thirty-five, young men and women finding our way.

I was the first in the hot seat. I had, perhaps foolishly, volunteered for it. I remember the blood pumping so hard through my neck it was difficult to hear what people were saying, and what I did hear I didn't like much. Someone to my left made a remark about sincerity. A lack of it. In my work. A lack of sincerity? I was outraged, though when things calmed down it turned out the remark had been directed at my spelling which, then and now, is pretty inventive. No real harm had been meant but it made it clear that the weekly sessions would always in some degree be personal, that we would all at some point be made uneasy by the scrutiny and hot breath of our peers. We decided to have a second meeting on the evenings following the scheduled and formal ones. We found a pub with a quiet upstairs room. Here we straightened things out and offered, when necessary, a little comfort and reassurance. It was a good recourse, and in that room our little group was perhaps at its best. We were not otherwise a vintage year, I think. Even nine can divide into cliques, sub-groups, splinters.

Our tutors were Malcolm Bradbury and then Rose Tremain. Malcolm I remember as an affable 'chair'. Pipe in fist, legs crossed, wearing (I think) a good thick jacket, possibly tweed, he let us have our say without interrupting us, and when we had talked ourselves into perplexity or (rarely) fallen silent and taken to staring at our toe-caps, he gathered up the threads and gave the discussion a sense of shape, of purposefulness. Did he, formally, teach us anything? I recall him once standing at the blackboard and chalking up a graph, x axis, y axis, a line climbing steeply between them. What this was intended to illustrate I have now no idea. Our future earnings? I fear not.

Rose handled us in similar fashion though she had no pipe nor (I think) tweed jacket. I found her slightly intimidating and have wondered since if she was happy at UEA or happy that year. Foolishly, I did not take up the opportunity to have a tutorial with her, something I still regret for she is a writer I admire immensely and one much closer to my take on things, my writerly sensibility, than Malcolm. I suspect I was afraid she didn't like my work and would say so. In truth, I didn't like my work much myself, and felt – or began to feel towards the end of that year – demoralised and frustrated. What had I achieved? A scattering of short stories, all very different, all very flawed. Yet looking back (across twenty years!) it seems to me that I was doing what I needed to, that I was trying things out, experimenting, doing the police in different voices. Had I been brave enough to have gone to my tutorial, Rose may well have commended such an approach.

In recent times I briefly joined the swelling (swollen?) ranks of writers teaching on Writing MAs, and was worried occasionally that the desire to get a 'good' MA makes some students cautious, clinging to whatever seemed to work for them in the past, nervous – understandably – of taking a chance with a piece of work that will go into formal assessment. The workshop system itself, where work in a fragile stage of development is subject to such close attention (even the spelling), may also have a limiting effect. But a readiness to take risks, a willingness to get it 'wrong', sets up in a writer precious

by Andrew Miller

habits of openness and audaciousness that will, in the long term, count for more than a distinction (I didn't get one) on a course, the non-vocational uses of which are fairly non-existent. As a reader I'm always more interested in ambition than competence. Aren't we all? The day we set out to write self-defensively, to play safe, we set out to make what, in Hollywood, they call 'product'. For those graduating in the pages of this anthology I wish something better, wish indeed what I wish for myself, a wilder ride in which we stubbornly attempt those things we fear might be beyond us.

....

A.M.

Prose Fiction

Introduction
by Henry Sutton

Joshua Bruce Allen
Gaynor Clements
Jack Davidson
Tom Raphael Eaves
Eluned Gramich
Jessica Granatt
Rebecca Tyng Kantor
Kate Macrae
Peter Matthews
Erin Meier
Anna Metcalfe
Will Miles
Claire Powell
Natasha Pulley
Eliza Robertson
Sara Sha'ath
Kim Sherwood
Dennison Smith
Siobhan Tumelty
Fuchsia Wilkins

Publishing is in a mess; the future of the novel at stake; the health of literary culture in jeopardy. Digitalisation is partly to blame. Amazon, possibly, more so. And then there are the publishers, in this country, in America, around the world who are imploding with insecurity and indecision. Indeed, never has it been harder to be a fiction writer, especially a writer of literary fiction. There's no market and no longer any clear or consistent means to bring work to the market. Yet here at UEA, on the Prose Fiction MA, we, the students and tutors, collectively, do nothing but nurture and champion the writing of fiction, nothing but encourage literary exploration, experimentation and extraordinary talent. Are we all mad? No, of course not. So is there any truth to this relentless literary doom and gloom? Depends who you listen to, where you look. What you want to hear.

Certainly, for as long as I've been published, now approaching two decades, people have been talking about the demise of the publishing industry – here, in the US, around the planet. We writers have always had the cards stacked against us. And still we've persisted with the writing, the honing of our skills, the mining of our experience, the stretching of our literary horizons. And still, too, works are published (variously), readers reached (somehow). Truth in fiction is what concerns us most.

There's no questioning the colossal changes taking place with regards to publishing, formatting and bookselling. Digitalisation is even beginning to influence issues of narrative, mostly through presentation, but also with regards to form, structure and intent. Suddenly, in this very new and ever evolving e-world, writers have so much more to grapple with than just words. While this year's students are keenly aware of the challenges and this swiftly (ever-) changing landscape, they are not overly daunted or any less determined to create fiction of serious and lasting value. They know what good fiction is, why it matters, why they want to write it, where it can take you, the seemingly endless possibilities – more now than ever. They

by Henry Sutton

have also discovered, I believe, that they are not alone. That together more can be achieved and sustained. We're all in this, having come some way, with energy, talent and commitment. There will always be a way to go (such is the unfolding drama of literary discourse, now coupled with rampant new technologies), but the writing in this anthology will give you some pointers, and plenty of heart.

....

H.S.

Joshua Bruce Allen

Get A Grip
A short story

'Nice place Louis has,' said one friend to another, over coffee.
'Yes,' she replied. 'Shame about the –' And she blushed and squirmed in her chair.

He nodded. 'It is rather unusual, isn't it?'

She took an empty sachet and folded it into a tiny triangle. When she became aware of his judgemental gaze, she placed it down carefully as if a conscious effort had been completed. 'I don't think I'll be going back,' she said.

'That's understandable,' he agreed. 'But he's such a dependable fellow.'

'Of course. A decent man, really, despite it all.'

They all agreed, Louis's friends, but they never said anything to him personally. Because what could reasonably be said, if he didn't know it himself? Surely he would have informed them if he was aware of it. And when a new member joined their circle and was invited to the flat, was it so naive of his friends to expect it to have been dealt with?

Clean, but not sparkling; neat, but not minimal; cold, but not freezing; the house had no independent character, it existed only in comparison. The thing of which his friends almost spoke was the exception. It might have been an erotic portrait in the hallway, perhaps a dog with chronic flatulence, but it was more elusive than either of these.

In the post-dessert lull, the tipsy conversation of the main course had descended into punch lines and soliloquies. Emma's calves were a little unco-ordinated, the heels didn't help, but she excused herself and made a graceful escape. Another guest had gone down the corridor earlier so she assumed that the bathroom was there. Some tasteful reproductions hung on the walls, generically Modernist in style. They were a blur of lines and colours in the bright light.

Only two doors were apparent. One was open and led into the kitchen. She opened the other to find a cupboard full of cleaning products. But then she saw a third door which she hadn't noticed. This must have been the bathroom. There was something odd about it which she couldn't put her finger on. She extended her arm to open it and turned – nothing! No handle! Shame boiled through her cheeks, accompanied by a vivid memory of performing a clarinet solo at a school assembly. The common factor in both situations was that she desperately needed to urinate, the urgency of which only inflamed her face further. Where the handle should have been was a hole, about two inches in diameter. She leant down to look inside. The axle to which the handle should have been fixed was slightly beyond the rim of the hole. Her fingers were numbed by alcohol and fumbling with fear. She touched the axle, but the hole was just too small and the axle just too far for her to grip it. Someone could have come down the corridor any minute, she couldn't let anyone see her like this.

An idea struck her: she'd seen an empty mop bucket in the cleaning cupboard. Before she could change her mind, she dashed in and hoiked her dress. The beating of a storm on a plastic roof, slowing to a few short taps. Crisis averted. She stood up and adjusted her clothes. If she left the bucket there, it would have been discovered. Trying to trick Louis into thinking he'd forgotten to empty the bucket wasn't an option; if there was one thing Louis was not, it was forgetful. On the other hand, someone could have seen her carrying the bucket to the kitchen sink. But there was no other choice. Emma took her heels off and listened carefully at the door. On a deep breath, she scurried out with the shoes and bucket,

by Joshua Bruce Allen

poured the piss down the sink and ran back. She adjusted the bucket to look exactly the way it was when she found it, put her heels on and stumbled back to the party.

Louis had grown up in a Kentish market town, the type where snootiness had evolved into a totalitarian regime. In this way it was a microcosm of the Garden of England, aside from the growing intrusion of Greater London. Preceding this horde came tabloid tales of stabbings and 'urban music', which had the same effect as the anti-morale leaflets once dropped by Axis planes: *Remember her last kiss? Gee, you were happy then ... together, you spent marvellous times ... lounging on the beaches ... dancing, enjoying parties galore ... listening to the tunes of your favourite band ... now it's SKEET SKEET SKEET! FIX UP, LOOK SHARP! BRAAP-BRAAP!*

He was sent to the local private school. There, with the help of Oxbridge-educated teachers, he achieved respectable, but not exceptional, results. He gained entrance to an elite university. His parents were proud. Only two generations ago they had been working class, and the new generation would be lawyers, doctors and architects. Louis graduated and passed his solicitor's exam then went straight into a London firm. Company law. Within six years he had gained a flat in a modestly affluent suburb.

On this morning his alarm sounded at seven thirty, as it did every morning. There was no distinction between working days and weekends. Within five minutes he was up and dressed in a pastel shirt, suit trousers and tie. He didn't shower, as this and other functions were performed at work or the gym near his flat if necessary. He ate a nutritious and filling wholegrain cereal with skimmed milk while watching BBC News. At quarter past eight it was time to leave. He put on his jacket and picked up his satchel. Before going, he checked his tie in the hallway mirror. The knot was slightly askew, but this wasn't the first thing he noticed; right there, on the middle of his own forehead, definitely present and in no way mistakable, was a round, metallic knob. A growth, slap on the front of his face! He looked away from the mirror and closed his eyes. When he looked back it would be gone, just a brief permeation of dreams into his day. He looked again; it was still there, bright as before! Louis had heard of people's hair turning white overnight, but this was in a league of its own. Hesitantly, he brought his hand towards it, his fingers hovering around the circumference. He touched it lightly with his fingertips. It was cold and smooth, like steel, with no nerves. Squeezing it, gently at first, he found it to be extremely hard. It was not hollow, as he discovered by tapping it with his pen.

His first thought was that there had been a dreadful nuclear disaster. Perhaps a contamination of the water supply. Probably everyone in London had one of these things on them, and he'd just been unlucky enough to get the facial variety. But why was there nothing on the news? To avoid a panic, of course. No need to get people riled up over a ... pimple. He would go the chemist on the way to work and everything would be fine. Even if the lump were benign, his medical insurance would cover this kind of cosmetic procedure.

As he walked down the street towards the underground, Louis was acutely aware of the lack of knobs on the pedestrians' heads, arms or legs. Was it likely that the knob of every person he passed in the street had appeared below the neckline? Perhaps the pathology of this disease favoured all parts over the head. He kept telling himself this as he entered the chemist.

'Good morning. I have a terrible spot, actually it might be a bite, on my forehead. Do you have some kind of cream?'

The girl behind the counter stared at him, slack-jawed. 'Does it hurt?' she asked.

'No, it's completely insensitive. Noticed it this morning.'

'I'll just speak with my colleague, give me a minute.'

She hurried behind the wall of bottles and coloured cartons. Louis looked in the mirror to the side of the counter and felt a strong urge to stroke the knob in the way that hirsute men caress their beards.

'Sorry, we can't help you. You should see a doctor.'

by Joshua Bruce Allen

He arrived at work as normal and was promptly sent home. In fact, he was given indefinite leave until such time as the knob had been removed. When it had not gone by the next morning, and was itself completely unchanged, he went to the doctor. At first the doctor thought that it was a body modification gone wrong. But when he saw that there was no scarring around the protrusion, no evidence whatsoever of external origin, he was convinced of Louis's story. An X-ray was arranged.

Louis had already organised another dinner party. His guests were surprised that he would entertain with his condition but he reassured them that it wasn't contagious, that he had been sent home for his own sake. Louis was pleased that Emma accepted his invitation. Ever since the last party he had held, she had ignored or rebutted him on every occasion. Whatever unintentional slight he had made must have been forgotten, he thought.

It was once again that time of the evening when bloated stomachs and diluted bloodstreams conspired to direct conversation down intricate paths to nowhere. Emma seemed to be in a strangely elevated mood, laughing hysterically at the tamest jokes and being friendly almost to the point of flirtation. She had been drinking noticeably more than everyone else, but it was hard to say whether this was cause or symptom of her abandon. Twice Louis noticed a glint in her eye when any mention of his condition was made. Had she come here merely to mock him? He could understand it if he knew what he'd done to offend her in the first place.

When Louis expressed his guilt at having to miss work, Emma grinned and said, 'Get a grip, Louis!' After which she laughed and downed half a glass of Cabernet Sauvignon. 'Get a handle!' she said, cackling even louder. Everyone must have been laughing at her, as there was nothing funny about what she'd said. Finally she stood up and, swaying to inaudible music, slurred, 'Get a knob!' and lunged at him over the table.

'Don't move!' she bawled, and grabbed it the second time. One hand holding the back of his head, she twisted the knob clockwise with a sickening crunch. A circular spray of blood, like covering the end of a hose with your thumb, doused Emma's dress and the tablecloth. Thin red snakes slithered from his nostrils. Levering herself against his body, the tendons showing in her arms and neck, she ripped the knob right off his head. Louis gargled crimson as a pink plug of offal slid down his cheek from the hole. He coughed pathetically and fell face first into his pavlova.

Emma wiped her face with the back of her hand, smudging spots of blood into war-paint stripes. She turned from the speechless guests and walked down the corridor to the door with no handle. The thin end of the knob fitted exactly into the hole and connected with the axle. She turned and pushed. Inside was impenetrable darkness. Her hands groped along the walls; there was no light switch. Typical.

....

Joshua Bruce Allen grew up in Kent and graduated from UEA with a first in English Literature and Philosophy. He has been published by Unthank Books and is writing a novel about a Roma Traveller who uncovers a conspiracy in the strange underbelly of Norwich.

by Joshua Bruce Allen

Gaynor Clements

Whistling The Devil
An extract from a novel in progress

Leah was checking trial bundles when she had her epiphany. She'd just made a start on bundle D, and was re-running her conversation with Kaye in the Rising Sun the night before, when it struck. Like a slap in the face that made her ears ring. The truth. The tying together of a thousand strands into one big knot of self-evident, obvious truth. Under her breath, all she could say was, 'Oh my God' and, 'Jesus Christ. Of course. Of course.' Ten minutes later, in the fifth floor Ladies, she was alternately splashing her face with cold water and staring at herself in the basin mirror when Kaye walked in.

'Thought I'd find you skiving in here,' she said. 'My God – are you all right?'

'As a matter of fact I'm not,' Leah replied with a calmness she didn't feel.

And two days later, in an act of beautiful symmetry, Cliff died.

*

As the train travelled towards St Albans the hills and hedgerows disappeared and sidings with heaps of shale and gravel took their place. Opposite Leah sat a woman who every now and then lifted her head from her book to gaze out of the window. Her pupils raced madly as they followed the flickering lines of buddleia growing alongside the tracks. Leah stared at herself in the window, searching her face as she would a stranger's. Her eyes began to sting. She saw the woman's reflection watching her and looked away.

The guard announced their arrival in fifteen minutes. Heads down, both women rifled in their bags for their tickets. She was very early; there was still an hour and a half before the service. Greg had asked if she wanted a lift and she'd refused, saying she could work on the train, but really she couldn't face them. Not now she knew and they didn't. She needed to get her head round it first.

'I can't understand what you want to go for anyway,' her mother said when Leah mentioned the funeral. 'He wasn't much of a father to any of you.'

She oriented herself using the map outside the station. She identified the church and taking her time she walked past the town's high street, with its ubiquitous shops, and along a 1930s ribbon development. Past empty houses full of shadows, waiting for people to return from work, kids from school. She walked down the hill and turned left, in front of a hardware shop that no one had been in for years, its window dominated by a saffron-coloured sheet behind the garden forks and cans of WD40.

She found the red brick Church of St Jude. It didn't even have stained glass windows. She paused, trying to find something of beauty and, finding none, carried on walking, round to the graveyard full of dandelions and headstones tilted at precarious angles. She knew she shouldn't, but she started down the path that ran down the middle of the churchyard, looking for the grave. It wasn't hard to find. Green tarpaulin lined the bottom and overlapped the sides, weighted down by rocks. A few worms struggled free of the nearby mounds of fresh earth. Gingerly, she stood on the edge and looked down.

Eventually, she made her way back to the church, past a small bin overflowing with dead chrysanthemums, and rusty watering cans used by relatives to fill the urns. Even the house of God has its mundane side, thought Leah.

Greg looked prosperous in his camel coat. He gave her a quick hug. 'How was the journey? Did you manage to rack up a few

by Gaynor Clements

chargeable hours?' June kissed her lightly. Her lips were cold. She wore a thin black cardigan which looked pilled and cheap. And Eve? 'She decided not to come after all,' said June. 'Well, she was only four when we left him, so what's the point?'

Leah kept quiet.

At they lowered Cliff into the grave, Greg was unmoved. June looked miserable at the best of times, so it was hard to tell what she was thinking.

*

The year they left him, Cliff entered some eggs in the Winsick Show. In the weeks preceding, he fed his bantams layers pellets, and the right amount of grit to stop them getting crop-bound. He gave them porridge with milk every morning and put vinegar in their water to strengthen the shells. On the day of the show he carefully carried six eggs wrapped in newspaper to keep them cool, all the way to Winsick. He even remembered to bring some straw and a plate for display.

He was confident. He carried Eve on his shoulders for most of the way and whistled *Smile For Me Diana* and *Scarlet Ribbons*, as they walked along roads lined with dry-stone walls and wild angelica.

The show was well under way when they arrived. Officious-looking men in white coats took notes on their clipboards and a man with a loudspeaker introduced the different breeds as they were paraded around the ring. Leah and the others milled around, past cows with brass earrings and plaintive faces, and tried to find something to buy at the stalls. By the end of the afternoon, they were all tired and thirsty and Eve had started to whinge. They perked up a bit as they went to check Cliff's entry. The exhibition tent was full of flies and smelled of hot cowpats. Long tables with white cloths were laid with raffia-tied onions and lanky runner beans. An egg from each of the entries in the 'Six Brown Eggs' class had been cracked to examine the colour and texture of the yolks. Cliff hadn't even managed third place.

He parked the kids outside the Black Swan with bags of crisps and bottles of pop and disappeared inside. Dusk was falling. The pub, built of the same stone as the walls that lined the fields, was old and full of dark corners. The notice outside said it had once been a resting post for Cromwell's men. 'You know this place is full of ghosts,' said Greg. 'Get lost,' said June. Eve started to cry. 'Yeah, shut up Greg,' said Leah. 'You're frightening them.' It was dark before Cliff came to tell them that someone had offered them a lift home.

When he got back that night, Cliff went straight to his allotment and wrung the necks of every one of his hens. He even dispatched the cockerel. 'No point in leaving you to go mad on your own,' he said as he twisted the bird's neck three hundred and sixty degrees.

*

After the service they crammed into the sitting room that Cliff had shared with his landlady. The carpet gave off a wet smell and every visible surface was covered in dust. Tall shelves dominated one wall, bearing not a single book, just some tiny ornaments out of scale with their surroundings. Beyond the shelves, through the window in the corner, Leah could see a tiny grey courtyard. Pots of leggy pelargoniums leaned against next door's fence, which bowed where the posts had rotted. The pinch-pleat curtains at the window drooped where they were missing hooks. Leah caught June's eye but she quickly looked away.

A glass vase of yellow chrysanthemums, their slimy leaves rotting in the water, stood in the centre of plates of curling sandwiches and pink wafer biscuits. The landlady's son offered round lumps of pastry with mushroom slime in the middle, which Leah suspected ought to have been served hot.

The landlady herself looked small and shrunken in her wheelchair. Her hair was a thin cloud of cotton wool through which Leah could see pink scalp. In her arthritic hands she held a sherry glass and an egg sandwich, neither of which she touched. At times she seemed almost to nod off.

by Gaynor Clements

And opposite Leah sat Mad Aunty Ivy. Leah had no real recollection of Ivy, but it was impossible not to know who she was. The Cullen cheekbones sat like crab apples under her powdered skin, and her pointed chin was just a smaller version of Cliff's. Ivy ignored them all, fixing on a spot past Leah's head, settling her face into a look which Leah couldn't place for a while, before deciding on spiteful stupidity.

Conversation was a muted murmur, as if people were afraid of startling the landlady from her stupor. Guests craftily checked their watches as they brought food to their mouths, calculating how many sandwiches stood between them and a polite exit. Leah made no pretence of any manners and chatted with Greg about his girls. June sat alone until the landlady's son began to make conversation from his standing position, forcing her to crane her neck upwards to catch what he was saying. A group of dark-suited, rough-looking men were arranged in a knot in the corner of the room. Apart from Leah and the others, and Ivy, there were no family members; certainly no one who resembled any of Cliff's seven surviving siblings.

Finally, Leah moved her chair to sit by the landlady.

'Hello. You must be Louisa?'

'Yes dear, that's me,' she said, slowly lifting her head from her chest.

'I'm one of Cliff's daughters. I live in London.'

'His daughter? Well now, I can see that one belongs to Cliff,' she said pointing at Greg. 'And that young girl there must be some relation. But you – I suppose you must favour your mother.'

Leah looked down at the landlady's puffy ankles. 'I have to get back soon, but I just wanted to say thank you for – for sorting things out.'

'That's all right dear. Someone had to do it. Even Cliff deserves a bit of a send-off.'

As they were walking back to Greg's car, June said, 'She likes the sauce as well, the old lady. Her son said her and Cliff knocked ten bells out of each other when they were pissed.'

'You're joking,' said Leah. 'She could hardly lift a sandwich let alone land a punch.'

'Just goes to show that nothing changes,' said Greg.

*

'He banked on me not having the guts with four kids in tow, but I showed him,' Josie used to say. And one night, after he'd gone to the pub, she piled everyone into a neighbour's Morris Minor and took them to their Grandma's. Mary's house was tiny, made more so by her refusal to let anyone use the Front Room. Very occasionally Leah would be allowed to take her Lego in there. The Front Room was as cold as charity, and the horsehair settee which overshadowed it was lumpy and hard and smelled of dust. Leah preferred to sit on the floor, that way she didn't get into trouble for messing up the antimacassars.

Not long after they'd arrived, Grandma was at the British Legion and Josie was on night shift, leaving Greg in charge. Leah was lying in the bed she shared with her mother and June, watching shadows of sprites and goblins flicker on the bedroom wall, when she heard Greg shouting, 'Why can't you just leave us be? Just get lost and leave us alone.' A man's low rumble said something in reply and then footsteps thudded up the narrow stairs. Greg followed, yelling, 'Get out. Get out. Get out.' The bedroom door flung open and Cliff lurched into the room. His black hair was wet with Brylcreem and his eyes looked glazed and faraway. He swayed for a second or two as he focused, then he took a few big strides towards the wardrobe and began to eviscerate floral-patterned dresses and tear the arms off pussy-bow blouses, which still smelled of her mother. Greg stood in the doorway hopping from foot to foot and wiping snotty tears on his mustard-coloured jumper. And all the time Leah lay, sheets pulled up to her nose, as if she were watching Santa Claus sneaking around the foot of her bed. Not once did Cliff look at her.

....

Gaynor Clements used to be a commercial lawyer in London, but has spent the last ten years looking after her two children. She has briefly escaped the cavernous maw of the laundry basket to undertake the Prose MA. She lives near Cambridge.

by Gaynor Clements

Jack Davidson

Buena Sombra
Extract from a novel

Morning has burned away quickly, the shade is warm. Robert is lying on the floor. He is surrounded by heat, and by the voices that echo around the crag. Some are recognisable, but there are others too. He'll find support if he begins. The climbers around him have a certain confidence. It's not something Robert understands. They smile as they begin their climbs. They're not strong. But they have something. Robert doesn't get it. Climbing doesn't make him happy. That comes afterwards. He has failed twice on the route that leers over him now. He's afraid to approach again, fearful of another failure.

'You going to give it another go?' asks Ueli.

Robert opens his eyes.

'Soon.'

He doesn't want to try again. He closes his eyes and hopes sleep will deliver him to the end of the day. High on the steep wall, there is a section that terrifies him. A good rest, a ledge. But the harder climbing is above. The rock is like polished wood in places, it offers his feet no security. He has retreated again and again to the ledge's safety. Ueli has been patient with him. He has given all morning to belaying, and Robert doesn't want to let him down. He has no excuse, but he has no motivation of his own. It is as if Ueli's enthusiasm for the climb only reaches to the ledge. Beyond it, Robert's alone. He opens his eyes. The landscape drops away to the river. He wonders how many of the climbers around the crag have even noticed it. Have they noticed that it flows out of the valley to olive groves in the distance? They probably haven't noticed the sweep of forest across the river either. It mirrors the crag like a garden mirrors its house. It's softer, inviting. Everything is an invitation to leave. Anything is more appealing than climbing. Climbing seems futile and pointless. It asks a lot, but there's nothing gained by it. Had he thought he would find answers at the top of some cliff? It's been six weeks since he left. He's no closer to going back – he isn't sure whether he can.

Lights in the kitchen. Silence. Robert's ears adjusted to it slowly after the car's engine. Jane's voice floated down the stairs. Sally's was more delicate, it took longer to detect. The sound of the door was distinct. They would have heard him come in. Robert called up to them anyway. Sally was stood at the top of the stairs in her pyjamas. Her hair wet and brushed. Robert's eyes came level with hers before he reached the top. Her small arms around his neck. She was warm. He continued upwards and her feet lifted off the floor.

'How did it go?' asked Jane.

'Later,' Robert said as he passed. He was quiet. He didn't want Sally to become involved. He didn't want her to have to hear worry in her mother's voice. He put Sally down on her bed.

He said, 'You're getting heavy. I won't be able to pick you up soon.'

She said, 'I think you will. Because you're strong' – she scrambled under the covers – 'Can I have a story?'

'Do you deserve one?'

'Yes.'

He reached down towards the bookshelf by her bed.

She said, 'No. A made-up one.'

He laughed, 'OK.'

Her arms stayed on top of the blankets, pressed at her sides. Her eyes were wide – she was paying attention. He didn't have the imagination for making stories up, but he was sure she hadn't heard *Goldilocks* before. He began with once upon a time; she liked his stories to start that way. The words settled her and she nestled further down into the duvet. He told her that once upon a time, there was a girl just like her. He could see she was desperate to ask why. But she knew well enough that if she remained silent, she would find out.

by Jack Davidson

She listened without moving. She fidgeted a little towards the end. Robert wondered whether she would be more interested if he were a better storyteller.

'What did you think?' he asked after finishing.

'I liked it. I liked the bears.'

'Not Goldilocks?'

'No, I don't think she's just like me at all. Not apart from her hair.'

He said, 'Why not?'

She said, 'Because she's not very nice. She steals their food and spits some of it out and breaks baby bear's chair.'

Robert laughed and said, 'I don't think she's much like you either.'

Sally smiled. It was the most beautiful smile.

He said, 'There is one thing though.'

'What?'

'Your bed. It's just right.'

As she nodded, her eyes were already closed. Her face held on to that final smile. Her breathing was soft. Jane had already closed the curtains. Between them, the glow of daylight was still visible. The clocks hadn't changed yet, summer was still there. When Robert was Sally's age, he would pretend to sleep until his mother or father had left the room. He would open his curtains and window. Later, he realised he could climb out into the garden. Nobody would notice. The last light of the day would be his. The freshness of it.

Robert stood slowly. Sally's sleep seemed so fragile that anything could wake her. He wanted to get outside before it was too late. He moved across the room and turned out the light without letting the switch click. Outside of the room, he breathed deeply. It was early in the evening still. He didn't want to relive the day explaining it to Jane. She was downstairs in the kitchen. Robert changed into a pair of jeans, a T-shirt. They were worn, but fresh after the suit. He'd never thought he'd wear a suit to work, but he'd settled into his job all too easily. He'd caught his reflection in a pane of glass one morning and realised he was in a suit. Settled down, married, a child. He looked down at the gold band on his finger. His hands had lost the brick-dust roughness they'd learned from his father. Even in a suit, he thought, a day's work is hard. But his only ache was the dishonest pain in the small of his back. It was all for Sally though. It was too late to change anything. He rolled up the bottom of his jeans and walked downstairs – the carpet soft under bare feet. The last hum of warm light was pouring in through all the windows. It filled the house. Jane was in the kitchen, opening a bottle of wine. With Sally in bed, the evening was theirs. Robert could forget work, and the meeting he'd come from.

Jane said, 'Is she settled down all right?'

'I told her a story,' said Robert.

Jane said nothing, she twisted the corkscrew into the bottle's neck.

'*Goldilocks.*'

Jane pulled at the cork. It wouldn't move. Robert reached out to offer a hand.

She said, 'I've got it.' She was sharp. The bottle between her knees. She was bent double, her elbow high. She forced the cork out. There was no control; the back of her hand swung out and hit the edge of the worktop.

'Fuck.'

'You'll wake Sally,' said Robert.

'Well close the fucking door then.' Her face was red, she was in pain. Robert closed the door and took the wine from her. He cradled her other hand, gently applied pressure to it. They parted a moment later.

She said, 'Thanks,' and smiled, 'would you like some wine?'

Robert looked out of the kitchen window. The light was excellent. The higher branches of the silver birch bathed in it.

'Let's sit in the garden with it,' he said.

'Now?' She looked shocked. She was wearing a pair of jogging bottoms, an old T-shirt. She'd say she looked a mess. But she shone through the clothes.

He said, 'It's lovely out there.'

She said, 'It's cold.'

He said, 'So put a jumper on.'

by Jack Davidson

And she said, 'I've had a long day, I just want to sit down and relax.'

He could have used the mess his day had turned into as leverage, but then he would've had to share the details. He would've worried her. Money would've become the issue.

He said, 'We can do that outside.'

'Rob, I don't want to. Let's just sit in the front room.'

Robert watched as the last light climbed higher up the tree. In the last moment it seemed the topmost leaves could hang on to it forever. And then it was gone. The garden still had a glow to it, but there would be no persuading her. She was settled, already walking out of the kitchen. He followed her, the stems of wine glasses crossed in his hand. In the front room, Jane drew the curtains and sealed out the darkening sky.

She said, 'So, how did it go?'

And it became unavoidable.

'OK,' Robert says. He stands. He's shaky but he tries to hide it, or ignore it. He will climb past the ledge and then fall. Get it over with. He will say that he isn't strong enough. He'll say that the route is impossible for him and put an end to the cycle of failure. With movement, the heat is back on him. He walks to the foot of the route. He feels hollow. His hands shake as he ties the rope.

'Ok?' Ueli asks. Robert turns to him, but Ueli just waits for him to begin.

'Yeah.'

'This time,' says Ueli – a small encouragement. Robert begins. He climbs out of the shade. It's easy. He reaches the ledge. A flake of smooth rock extends around it like a bell. Robert catches his breath. He knocks against the flake. This shade is cool, a different shade to the one he has been laid in. But he must leave the security. He steps around onto the side of the bell, finds the pathetic hold on top of it. There's a plant growing there. He hadn't noticed it last time. It points to a deep pocket in the rock, reached easily. He steps back out onto the face, out into space it feels. This is where he'll fail. This

Buena Sombra

onto the face, out into space it feels. This is
will be the end to it. A shallow dish in the ro
He must navigate past it. He holds himself
releases his right gradually from the security o
slowly, with the care of a surgeon. He dare
meet and he switches his feet on a tiny, glassy hold.
are a fight. He doesn't know what will come next. The wall above is steep. But he presses on with a new confidence. He's climbed above his expectations. He is outside of himself. Looking on as he breathes through the next move, and the next. He is unstoppable. The chains that mark the end of the route come too soon, just as it becomes effortless. He lowers back to the floor without taking his eyes off that dish. It was as if a switch had been flicked. The fear had left him, and something else had taken over. He finally understands. The effortlessness of it – he wants more. Before he reaches the floor, there is a satisfaction he has never known before – to have given everything and succeeded. A few more seconds of weightlessness. He's happy. There is nothing else.

Ueli feeds out the last bit of rope. Robert had forgotten him, forgotten for a moment there even was a rope. There was the rock, the perfect movements that it asked for. Nothing more. He wants to tell Ueli that he understands. But he says nothing. Ueli nods, he doesn't need telling. There's a smile between them – it says everything that needs to be said.

....

Jack Davidson is from Lincolnshire. He is currently working on a novel about a man who abandons the responsibilities of work and family, and discovers rock climbing as a means to reinvent and test himself.

by Jack Davidson

from Raphael Eaves

Josephine Primitive
Extract from a novel

Horns blared by the dozen: a rare windless day at the start of the high season, stop-starting in the hot mid-morning traffic on the road into Bigtown. I had the AC blowing at gale force with the windows rolled down; the heat and stink inside was the same as out, but it was moving.

Outside on the hard shoulder the shirtless drunks were loping back and forth, swinging forty-ounce bottles by their necks, waving their long dusty arms at each other, staring down the passing cars with angry, salmon-pink eyes. This was the tradition of the a.m: by noon, all the drunks – except the totally drunk or deranged – would drag themselves into the shade.

Up ahead a sewage suction truck was blocking both lanes; muscled Joes in muck-spattered Hi-Vis wrestling a thick green hose like a live anaconda.

It was 1997, it was Valentine's Day, and St Joseph was drowning in shit. Those of us that washed were doing so with bottled water: from our faucets and showerheads came nothing more than a rasping death rattle, sometimes a brownish sludge like smooth peanut butter. Swimming pools bloomed with algae, then evaporated.

The water supply – according to Health and Sanitation Department notices peeling from walls and fence posts all over the island – remained an irremediable soup of parasites, pathogens, oils and greases, pesticides and general run-off from the streets and sewers.

It was the hangover from Janet: a cat 4, downgraded at the last possible moment to a cat 3: the price we paid for a lucky escape.

She'd reared up out of the Atlantic in late November and had been predicted to tear the roof off every house on St Joseph, to steamroll prefabs and smaller residences and kill or maim anything that did not run for cover. The coastline took a serious bath in the preceding storm surge but Janet died mysteriously over the Barclay Islands, only grazing us in her final death throes. The worst of it took out the St Chris ferry building and levelled a swathe of the Port Neville shantytown.

But the coastal surge and heavy rains had already flooded the island's sewage treatment plant, and all kinds of ungodly shit had started pouring back into the drains, the streets, back into the water supply. Then came outbreaks of diarrhoea, Hep C, dysentery – even a report of cholera at a four star resort in Sugar Garden Bay. Not even the poorest Joes drank Josephine tap water, but these new poisons, the Health and Sanitation notices shouted in blood-red lettering, could kill you through your skin.

But it didn't mean much to the drunks on the hard shoulder, nor to the Hi-Vis Joes, nor the Joes honking in their shamelessly modified vehicles. Nothing more than a reverberating stench, a writhing hose, boys humping 5-gallon cooler bottles along the roadside.

By February it was 29°C and we were still washing with bottled water. Our drinks were served without ice.

Even the sea had been declared off limits. As a rule the Joes steered clear of the water; some half-forgotten superstition turned instinct. But for us residents – and the more intrepid turkeys – this was largely ignored: the sea belonged to us.

Finally clear of the foul-smelling suction truck the traffic catapulted out the other side of Bigtown, passing through its outer ring of supermarkets and used car showrooms. From there all the way to St Joseph International Airport the roadside was a scrolling parallax of empty lots; boneyards for disused farm and industrial machinery left to rust in the damp air, beset by weeds and streaked with bird shit. It was nothing, a place between places, but St Jo was so small that even nothing was something. They called it the Dead Ground, although it was more unfinished than dead, like whoever

by Tom Raphael Eaves

built St Joseph had run out of time, or materials, or enthusiasm. The only milestone on the Dead Ground – apart from the transient evangelicals and their circus-top marquees – was the listing skeleton of the Brierly plantation, cut in half by a ragged chain link fence, and beyond it the giant corrugated box of the Josephine rum distillery.

Up ahead SJI's clapboard control tower began sprouting from the shimmering dirt. The airstrip was large enough to be serviced only by 15-seater turbo-props that hopped between St Christopher and the Barclays, the Piper Cubs chartered to the Pear Island Resort, the occasional Navy Hercules, dropping like carrion crows onto the tarmac.

Where the road skirted the airport's high fences I spotted one of the little wind-up turbo-props coming in over the sea: the midday flight from St Christopher, carrying my brother John home again.

From the air, you wouldn't know that St Joseph was drowning in shit. Looking down as you banked over Waking Island for the final descent, if you managed to overlook the frowsy concretion of Bigtown, the rathole scrimmage of Port Neville, then St Joseph might appear to you like a child's drawing of an island paradise: lush, volcanic, ringed with aquamarine.

I pulled up in the taxi rank in front of the terminal building and John was already stood outside, smoking, towering above the agitated crowd of turkeys.

He'd put on weight. The skin around his nostrils and lips was cracked and red and there were purple kidney-shaped bags under his eyes. His hair, once buzzed into a martial crew cut, was long and greasy and haphazardly tied back with some kind of black velvet scrunchie, the kind a young girl might use. He was dressed in a lime-green Tommy Bahama shirt, stained white shorts and a pair of plastic flip flops. It was a classic turkey getup, or what our father might wear on Sundays around the compound.

I climbed out of the Jeep and waded through the pallid sea of turkeys, who were fanning themselves with flyer-sized versions of the contamination notices as they queued to be loaded onto resort buses, shepherded by Joes in short-sleeved uniforms and matching caps. John spotted me but he acted like he hadn't, taking long, studied drags on his cigarette, waiting for me to come to him.

He had only one small bag with him, on rollerblade wheels. We stood for a while in silence, smiling at each other just a few feet apart, John smoking in that old affected way, breathing in the humid Josephine air with all that smoke. He looked at home, which is what he was. St Joseph was all I'd ever known – I belonged to its moist folds, its heavy press of weather, its glutinous warmth. But John, despite his boomerang velocity, was really a part of it. He was a blood relation of its hot garbage, its menagerie of feral dogs and poultry, the oily hum of generators at night.

'It's all the same,' he said, looking past me, past the sweat-soaked turkeys in their groaning coaches and minivans. From where he was standing John couldn't see much more of St Joseph than the taxi rank, the car park, the distant shape of Brush Mountain rising above a rotten billboard advertising Josephine rum, but it was true: he'd been away for a year – his most successful attempt at leaving yet – and St Joseph had hardly changed.

In central Bigtown there was now a MacDonald's, and adjacent to it a brand new art deco style cineplex that towered, peach-coloured and windowless, over Bigtown's three-storey skyline. In the old town square the offices of Jarrels & Bork Financial Services – where our father Rudolph had worked for twenty years – had recently been painted pistachio green, and had taken over the old court building next door. Rudolph had suffered a heart attack while playing squash and had died two thousand feet over the Caribbean Sea; our mother had started drinking in the early afternoons and was amassing a cortège of stray dogs, plucked from back streets and hill roads and from outside restaurant kitchens. But John was right: everything was the same as it was. Like St Jo was only waiting for John to come home.

As we pulled out of the taxi rank he retrieved a pair of red anodised shades from his shirt pocket, and squeezed them onto his head. They were aerodynamic, the lenses mirrored and luridly iridescent; although they concealed his eyes, they stressed the purple cushions underneath.

by Tom Raphael Eaves

'So the old chariot's still going strong,' he said.

Up ahead there had been a mild collision between a resort coach and a Joe with a mobile food cart. The cart-pusher was stood quarrelling with the driver, the turkeys peering down pale-faced through the blue-tinted windows. As a bored-looking Joe policeman waved us into the contraflow, John leant his swollen torso out of the window and gave the turkeys a royal wave. 'Look at this big man over here,' said John as we picked up speed, lighting another Independent off the end of the last. 'Christ, you must have the longest hair in St Jo. And what's with all the black? You must be boiling alive.'

'Not really.'

'So you're a Goth now?'

'No.'

'So you cut your arms?'

'No.'

'Mutilate cattle?'

'Not recently.'

'You could burn down one of the Dead Ground big tops. I'll help.'

He slung his meaty arm over the door, letting it hang over the cockeyed centreline, his cupped hand shielding the cigarette and almost brushing the cars and trucks speeding past the other way. We drove in silence past the Josephine distillery, past the severed remains of the Brierly Plantation and the sagging domes of the transient churches.

We crawled into central Bigtown, its continuous sonic chew and stomp: Reggaeton blared from every car, every doorway and window; a maddening doppler effect; clonal anthems beating each other down in the solid heat. That week it was Tego Calderón, El General, Nando Boom, interrupted only by the sticky, marshmallow strains of Tonelle Washburn; the one the Joes called Conqueror, El Ambasador.

To combat the noise outside, John hit the tape player, and Slayer vibrated his pack of Belizean Independents off the dash. Swearing, he switched to the radio, and tuned it until he found one of the local stations playing salsa, digital gospel and cheap Latino country music. He rifled through the tapes scattered on the dash, metal mostly, a

Josephine Primitive

few of John's old tapes; Beastie Boys, Public Enemy, the earliest of them recorded straight off MTV through my Fisher-Price tape recorder. They were the soundtrack to the countless laps we'd made around the island, John driving and Gus – his twin, older by seven minutes – timing him on a stopwatch. Back then my presence was barely tolerated in the Jeep, just enough to bounce around mutely on the back bench, trying to keep up with their back-and-forth over the perpetually alien music, watching the cigarette smoke curling round the backs of their identically stubbled heads.

John gave up on the tapes, and lit yet another cigarette. In between songs the DJ gabbled on in the same cartoonish, amplified Josephine Creole shared by every radio DJ on the island: a tawdry, lilting drawl knocked together from bits of Spanish, English, French, even faint echoes of the old tongues; the pre-Columbian whooping carried eight hundred miles from Venezuela in dugouts and pig-skin canoes.

Finally we passed the sewage treatment plant on the outer limits of Bigtown, where fat Joes with clipboards and dark bibs of sweat soaking through their short-sleeved shirts were waving their arms at skinnier Hi-Vis Joes wearing paper respirators, and continued up into the relative cool of the hills on empty roads. John switched off the radio and the only sounds were the Jeep's engine, the crunch of gravel and refuse under the wheels, the sough of the wind as it screwed into the steep, forested slopes.

'I need a drink,' said John. 'White Sails?'

'They're waiting for us.'

'It's been a year,' he said. 'They can wait a little longer.'

....

Tom Raphael Eaves is 24 and from London. He's the recipient of the Jerwood/Arvon Mentoring Prize and the Malcolm Bradbury Memorial Bursary. His novel *St Joseph* is set on a Caribbean island during the 1997 hurricane season.

by Tom Rapheal Eaves

Eluned Gramich

Untitled
Extract from a novel

Mooragh Camp, Isle of Man, 1945

I wasn't always on this island. There was a time where I was a German in Germany and a time where I was a German in England, and neither were particularly good to me. I came to the country in the autumn of 1937. It was my older sister, Annette, who sent me. She wrote to a cousin of my mother's, Charlotte, who had married an Englishman, an engineer by the name of Davidson. He'd worked in Duisburg, in the factories, decades earlier, where Charlotte had been a typist. We'd never met this relation, neither my sister nor me, since she'd emigrated when our mother was still unmarried.

In her letter, Annette said I was *ambitious, eager to experience life in another country.* I didn't recognise the young man whom Annette described. The only things I recognised were the facts: that I was Robert Fuhrmann, eighteen years old, and an apprentice in metalwork. Everything else was alien to me, a distorted version of my character.

My sister expected a rejection. So did I. Instead, we received a kind-hearted reply, not only offering me a room and board, but also letting me know there was a junior position available at the Bristol Airplane Company where her husband worked. She even went as far as to include a note of gratitude to us, since – in her words – *Carl has been inundated with orders of late and is in dire need of an extra pair of hands.* Considerate enquiries after my mother's health followed.

Annette read the letter aloud to me in the sitting room. We sat next to each other on the sofa, enjoying the quiet hours after school, before Heinrich returned from the office. I didn't agree to the plan at first, but I reconciled myself to the idea at supper while watching my brother-in-law wolf down his potatoes, an over-sized napkin protecting his uniform from splatters of cream sauce.

The day I left, Heinrich said goodbye to me early in the morning. He shook my hand for the first time and wished me 'all the best'. My sister brought me to the station in a cab and paid for a valet to take my luggage. On the platform, she handed me an envelope with money and said, 'From Heinrich'. I hesitated, but she stuffed the envelope into my jacket pocket and said, 'Don't be silly.' She waved me off. I know it's absurd, but I was disappointed she didn't cry. In fact, as the train pulled out of the station, I even imagined she looked a little relieved.

Charlotte Davidson was younger than my mother, and unlike her, she had a slim, steely body and abrupt manner, quite at odds with the polite tone she'd adopted in her letter to us. She was the kind of woman who always seemed to be doing something: cleaning the tabletops or rearranging the kitchenware. She did not indulge in friendships, or any fanciful pleasures. When she greeted me, she hardly said a word beyond, 'I hope you like a good beef stew', before vanishing into the back of the house. After a while, I came to understand that her behaviour was a manifestation of shyness rather than personal dislike. I grew used to it, and even liked her for it.

Carl Davidson was very different to his wife: he was a good-humoured man, bald, but with a large, grey moustache and a pair of heavy spectacles which he liked to take on and off. I'd been anxious about meeting him, more so than meeting Charlotte (at least she spoke German). I shouldn't have been worried. He was fascinated by me. On the night of my arrival, he sat me down and plied me with spirits and cigarettes, transforming the lounge – a tired, empty place – into a gentleman's smoking room. He asked about the journey: how Duisburg had changed since he'd been there. I tried my best to entertain him with stories of my childhood and apprenticeship. I tried to describe my sister's character ('gentle', I said, 'patient'),

by Eluned Gramich

and he encouraged a lengthy description of my mother's bad health, forcing me to tell the long story about her stroke; how she could no longer talk, eat unaided or wash herself.

'Your sister is a saint,' Carl said. He spoke English slowly for my benefit. Even then I could detect the lazy 'rs' which I later knew to be features of a Bristolian accent. 'My mother was the same. She suffered terribly from a swelling of the brain. It was Charlotte who took care of her. Passed away two years ago now.'

I could only nod. I was tired from my journey. I felt myself slip away from the conversation, even though I wanted to be as amiable as I could. 'A diligent folk, the Germans,' he went on. A sentiment he often repeated. 'I love the German people. As you can see, I married one of them.'

I set down my cigarette and rested my eyes.

'You must be absolutely exhausted.' His voice reached me from afar. I smiled weakly.

Charlotte showed me to my room: a snug, narrow bed, a writing desk and window overlooking the garden. When I opened the doors to the wardrobe, my shirts already hung there, fresh and ironed, all in a row. To the right of my shirts hung four infant christening gowns, the white delicate lace illuminating the dark corner.

The Davidsons lived in a large, Victorian house with several bedrooms. They had three grown-up daughters who'd all left home, and each room contained some trace of female presence: pieces of half-finished embroidery, knitting needles, women's clothing folded but not yet put away. Charlotte flitted through the house, picking things up, claiming it as 'Emma's' or 'Adelaide's'. 'Leave it there,' she'd say. 'It's Georgia's. Leave it. I'll deal with it.' The youngest daughter had only recently left: the door to her bedroom remained shut, untouched. She'd married an accountant and moved to his family home in Keynsham. The other two lived further away, in London. Davidson talked about 'the girls' as if they were children who'd gone on a school trip. 'I'll tell Georgia when she comes', he might say. I never met any of their daughters; not even the youngest, as she was busy settling into married life. Charlotte would make large dinners, enough potatoes and carrots to feed twice the amount of people. She'd always encourage me to eat more.

'It'll only go to waste,' she said. 'You need it. A growing lad like you.'

'Leave him be if he doesn't want it. Stop wasting money on all this food,' Carl said, smiling. Beneath the smile, there was a glint of reproach. Carl did not like to see money spent where it shouldn't. Charlotte ate very little, fidgeted at mealtimes, wiping the table with a damp cloth, rubbing at spots of dirt only she could see.

The language of the household was English and I learnt quickly. Charlotte would, on rare occasions, whisper a German phrase, here and there, like a grandmother slipping money into a child's pocket. My school English blossomed into language: the funny drawling vowels flowing from my mouth with increasing ease. I did not sound like myself anymore. I sounded better, closer to that *ambitious young man* my sister had wanted. Carl delighted in giving me 'practice sentences' – tongue twisters and points of elocution. Although Carl himself did not speak like the radio broadcasters, in his lessons with me he adopted the same inflated, kingly tones.

By studying the English language, I also learnt a lot about my own. German is a language of feeling. It assumes there is something else, beyond the grammar and syllables, which is failing to be conveyed. And so words are fabricated, stitched together, like a production line, in the attempt of trying to nail down an ineffable quality. English, on the other hand, assumes speech has no such purpose: language is there to pass the time, to be enjoyed for its own sake. Carl loved punning, for instance. A thorn in my side, punning. What did it matter if a word had more than one meaning? He took joy from simply pointing out, as if saying, 'Look, this is nonsense.'

The only extended German conversation I had in the time I was in Britain was one dreary weekday evening, when Carl was out on a social call. I'd opened my bedroom door to see that Charlotte had ironed my clothes and hung them neatly in my wardrobe. I went

by Eluned Gramich

looking for her in the house to thank her and, in part, to seek out company in the stormy winter weather. The house was so big and empty: it was eerie to sit alone in the lounge without Carl in the evenings.

I found Charlotte in the kitchen, bowed over the counter, peeling vegetables for the next day.

'Thank you,' I said.

'For what?'

'For cleaning my things.'

'My pleasure,' she replied, still engrossed in her task. She did not look round; perhaps she would have preferred to be alone, but I wasn't ready to leave.

'Weather's bad,' I went on.

'Yes.'

Sheets of rain struck the window. I didn't want to go back to the lounge. I fancied it was warmer in the kitchen. I thought about the shirts, so carefully starched and ironed, all in a row.

'Why are there four?' I asked.

'Four what?'

'Four christening gowns.'

'Oh.' She looked up. She pulled down her sleeves, did up the cuffs. 'Didn't Carl say?' she said, in German this time. I shook my head. 'We had four children. The last one we had was a little boy. Carl Gottfried.'

'Same as father,' I said, unthinkingly.

'It's a family name. My father, your great-uncle, was also Gottfried.' Charlotte turned slightly towards me, looking over her shoulder. German softened her speech. I heard my sister Annette's voice in the familiar inflections.

'What happened to him? The boy, I mean.'

'The little one,' she said quietly. The sweet phrase hung in the air between us, *the little one*. Then she seemed to pull herself together. 'Oh, he died.' She turned her back to me again. 'One night he started coughing and there was nothing we could do to stop it. It's the way things are sometimes. The Lord took him. He didn't belong in this

Untitled

world.' She slowed, and added, 'I had the feeling that he wouldn't stay, even when I was carrying him. I had the feeling …'

She shook her head, took up the chopping knife and started to slice the carrots for the broth. I felt like I was intruding on a private grief now that I had discovered it. I did not know what to say. The silence lengthened, marked only by the sound of the knife on the board. I got up to leave. As I opened the kitchen door, she called after me, 'Don't tell Carl.'

'What do you mean?'

'What I said about feeling our son wasn't going to stay with us. Don't tell Carl. It will only upset him.'

Eluned Gramich was born in Wales and grew up speaking Welsh and German at home. She studied English at Oxford. She was shortlisted for the Bristol Short Story Prize 2011 and is currently working on her first novel.

by Eluned Gramich

Jessica Granatt

Sanjil, Boom Boom
Extract from a short story

The light here is luminous and hazy as if filtered through smoke. The sky is a dead, matte blue. Sarah can smell cooking oil, petrol fumes and tobacco. Faintly beneath all that, she can smell the sea, which is dark and quiet and laps at the tiled wall of the café. The water is four feet from her, but the air is too thick to taste of salt. The word *hot* is not enough. Nobody here sweats: the heat doesn't let moisture sit. Where sunlight hits her, Sarah feels her skin parch. Shirtless men fish on the rocks. Boys take turns throwing themselves off the jetty, their wet feet smacking the boards, their bodies glistening. Patrick stares out at a tanker hulking far from the harbour. The cuffs of his shirt are unbuttoned, his single act of surrender. Sarah tries to meet Patrick's gaze behind his sunglasses. His guidebook is placed on the table between them.

'How are you feeling now?' asks Sarah.
'Fine,' says Patrick. 'Can't complain. I've been horribly ill.'
'You said,' says Sarah. 'It's the water.'
'Sensitive digestion,' says Patrick.
'Flat Coke,' says Sarah. 'Still, if you're feeling better, let's get food.'
'It comes and it goes,' says Patrick. He shifts about in his seat.
'Well, which one is it?' says Sarah.

They are talking quietly, but people still look. There are, of course, not many tourists in the city. Sarah feels that everybody in the café is watching her. A small child is the most blatant. He squirms and twists in his chair, stares right at her eyes. Two young women are sitting together behind Patrick. They giggle over coffee served in green glasses. Giggling at *her*, Sarah is inclined to think. One wears hijab, the other does not. Both wear glittering dresses and have beautiful, thickly made-up faces. Sarah feels drab, embarrassed by her rucksack. At the back of the patio old men smoke nargileh. They seem more interested in the girls than in Sarah and Patrick.

The waiter comes over. 'Bonjour,' he says. 'Welcome, welcome. You wanna drink? Wanna eat?'

Sarah goes to speak, but Patrick interrupts. 'Coke. And nargileh,' he says, loudly and slowly. 'You want a pipe, right?'

'I thought you felt sick,' says Sarah. 'Aren't you hungry?'

'My body cannot handle any more bloody hummus,' says Patrick.

'We have fuul, shawarma, shish taouk.'

'Fuul please,' says Sarah. The waiter keeps staring at Patrick. 'Excuse me?' she says. 'Fuul and tea please. No sugar.'

'Sugar,' says the waiter.

'Fine, shukran,' she says. The waiter is delighted.

'Ahlan, ahlan!' he says. 'You are so welcome!'

The holiday has not gone well, though Sarah had high hopes. It was too much of a risk, she thinks now. They've only been together a few months. She has tried hard to understand Patrick. Hours of effort. But the more trouble he is, the more she wants. So here they are; two weeks of lagging in cafés, clutching at topics. His appeal is unclear. She likes him for stupid traits she would find dislikable in others, which makes her think this must be The Real Thing. Otherwise what?

The waiter comes back to prepare the pipe. He puts a scrawled receipt down on the table. Patrick does not move to act until Sarah's fished for a note. She pays, trying to hide her misgivings.

'I'll get it next time,' Patrick says. Too late, thinks Sarah. He gets the charcoal going and the air between them is soured. We are failing, thinks Sarah.

Those of her friends who have been allowed to meet Patrick marvel at the task of him. They cannot fathom why she'd bother. The day Sarah decided she liked him, she took to paying attention. She laughed if he was funny and even if he wasn't, which made her hate herself in a small way. Still, it worked; Patrick wasn't used to

by Jessica Granatt

somebody caring and was flattered. Then he began sharing his asides with her. They pretend it was always like that. Complicity became intimacy.

There is one other couple in the café, sitting properly, facing. They gaze eye-to-eye with open, artless joy. Sarah doesn't feel envy. She tends to see things in the extreme long term. These people will all get left, she thinks, in one way or another.

Patrick is suddenly animated. He gabbles in an excited whisper.

'My God, have you seen that? Ten o'clock by the door. No, don't look now, for fuck's sake.'

Sarah waits then turns, pretends to get something from her bag. 'Bloody hell,' she says. 'And I worry.'

'From Beirut, I guess,' says Patrick.

'What kind of a place,' says Sarah. 'You can't wear a bikini, but you can pay to get sliced up.'

'At least she's never going to drown,' says Patrick.

'Where's her confidence?' says Sarah. 'Where's her self-esteem?'

'Oh, I can see them,' says Patrick.

'Go over', says Sarah. 'If you find her so compelling.'

'Calm down' says Patrick. 'It's a freak show. You know I'm not into that. I'm with you, aren't I?'

Sarah excuses herself to the toilets. She wants to pee but cannot, because it is one of those holes in the ground with a hose and no paper. She puts on lipstick, then reconsiders, tries to rub it off. When she's done, she stands in the indoor part of the café and watches Patrick watching the woman. It is cooler in here, in the dark, with the fans. There's a TV fixed up in the corner, stuck on a news channel she can't understand. It churns out footage of explosions happening somewhere. The waiters all stand around.

Patrick carries on staring at the woman from Beirut. She has a tight face, scar tissue shiny. He wonders what it would feel like not to be entirely flesh. Fake breasts do not slump to the sides when lain down: this he knows from porn, not experience. Would they be a hindrance during CPR? Patrick remembers an article about implant migration, some cowboy plastic surgeon. He imagines British silicon sacks squeezing out their owners. Maybe via the mouth. *We are heading for sunnier climes,* they'd say, plopping into the channel. They'd swim in formation.

Sarah comes back out. 'Why are you laughing?' she asks.

'Did you know implants could migrate?' Patrick says.

'Let's just fucking switch seats, if they're that much of a distraction.'

'Imagine it. Every winter, them all buggering off to Cape Town.'

Sarah smiles. 'I think migration, I think Serengeti.'

'I never made it through *Planet Earth*,' says Patrick. 'Attenborough can be a cold-hearted bastard.'

'Well you can't interfere,' Sarah says. 'He does the right thing.'

Sarah's fuul arrives and she eats, spearing the beans with a cocktail stick. Lemon and cumin and salt. Patrick gets hungry.

'Do you want some shisha?' he asks.

'I don't think women do that here,' she says. 'I don't want to offend anyone.'

Patrick laughs sarcastically. 'I'm going to get some eggs or something. You want anything?'

'Arak,' says Sarah.

Inside, Patrick has trouble getting served. Everybody seems very distracted. He wonders whether they mind that he wants alcohol. But if it was a problem, why would they stock it?

Sarah stays at the table while Patrick orders his food. The waiter comes over with ice and glasses. The ice slides about on the plate. Sarah takes a cube and presses it to her forehead. She considers her face in the reflection of her glass. She is not beautiful. Her jaw is set too heavy. The sort of woman who'd get described as handsome, in a book. But she knows she's just plain. Her body's shapeless. How much would it cost to get something done here? Cosmetic tourism, it's called. She heard about it on Radio 4.

Patrick sits back down. Sarah studies him carefully. 'What would you get done?' she asks. 'To your body. Limitless funds.'

'Something stupid,' says Patrick. 'A prehensile tail. Lobster pincers.'

by Jessica Granatt

'That's you all over. A weirdo. Though a tail would be fun.'
'If I'm so weird,' says Patrick, 'why are you with me?'
'I like you,' she says. 'I find you endearing.'
'And you?' says Patrick. 'Abdominoplasty? Collagen fillers?'
'Nothing,' says Sarah.
'Liar,' says Patrick.
'It's a moral stance,' says Sarah.
'Liar,' says Patrick.

As Patrick eats, Sarah watches the boys splashing in the water. They take turns running up the jetty and dive-bombing each other.

'What's up with their skin?' asks Patrick.
'What do you mean?' says Sarah.
'Are they burnt or something? They're all weird and shiny.'
'Suncream, maybe,' says Sarah.
'There's oil on the water,' says Patrick. Sarah sees the black surface glimmer.

'Well that explains the smell,' she says. 'That's not good. Someone should really sort that out.'

As the sun dips, the café gets darker, but not cooler. Patrick and Sarah listen to the drone of the Maghrib adhan tangling through the city. Some customers leave for Mosque. Throughout the trip, Sarah has found the call to prayer beautiful and comforting, but tonight it makes her feel very far from home. By the time it fades, the women have all left. More men arrive. They do not sit at the tables, but go straight inside. Patrick and Sarah do not pay attention. They order another pipe, more Arak. When the gunfire starts, the waiter laughs because they judder. Patrick pales.

'End of school,' the waiter says. 'Everybody gets excited.'
'I will never get used to it,' says Sarah.
'You can get used to anything,' says Patrick.

Sarah, now a bit drunk, feels a need to confide. She's pretty sure they'll break up once this so-called holiday is over, and would like to offload as many unwanted emotions as possible on him before then.

She says, 'I can't take this pressure. I'm a Western woman. Liberated, autonomous. But you know what? I'd rather be beautiful. Just sexually appealing to more people.'

'Wouldn't we all?' says Patrick. 'There's no shame in that. So you don't get what you want, boohoo.'

'It's not the same,' says Sarah.

'Everybody's scared of rejection,' says Patrick. 'It takes guts.'

'Every time I am rejected, it is more than personal,' says Sarah. 'It takes me so far from the definition of what I'm meant to be. You wouldn't understand.'

She turns her head away from him and gazes out at the water, imagining her silhouetted profile on a cinema screen.

'Keep your sad shit to yourself,' says Patrick. 'Don't bring me down. Why wouldn't I understand? You think it's really that different? Dwell on your strengths.'

'I could never pull off predatory,' Sarah says. 'I'll go along with smart and innocent and I'll get men like you. But then what if nothing works when I am old? I'm not meant to be scared of being old and alone.'

'Who says?'

'Third wave feminists.'

'You actually worry about them?'

'Feminism benefits me, as a smart, plain person. Not women, collective. Just me.'

'The only feminists you can trust are the beautiful, married, successful ones,' says Patrick. 'They alone don't have an agenda.'

From across the water they hear the soft boom of an explosion, followed by a shower of rain-on-tin gunfire.

'This is pretty loud,' says Sarah. 'It's worse tonight.'

'Probably fireworks. It's Friday,' says Patrick. Sarah nods in agreement. Inside the café the voices are raised, then the voices go

by Jessica Granatt

silent. The men all stare at the television, but the electricity cuts. All the men throng out of the café and leave very quickly. The younger ones pile onto mopeds in twos and threes. Sarah and Patrick watch as flashes of light bounce around the harbour. A plume of smoke rises. Patrick beckons to the waiter.

'What's going on?' he asks. 'No trouble, little trouble. Angry men, no problem. More Arak?'

'Can I smell fire?' Sarah says.

'Just souk, angry people. You know, problems.' The waiter gestures widely with his hands. He does a big shrug.

Jessica Granatt was born in Kent in 1987. Before coming to UEA, she studied English at UCL and French at the Sorbonne. She is currently working on her first novel.

by Jessica Granatt

Rebecca Tyng Kantor

Kitsch
An excerpt from a novel

Philadelphia, 1946

Erna's father had a headache, so Erna and Klaus set out for the Blooms' tea on their own. It was late December, almost Christmas. Near Rittenhouse Square, horse-drawn sleighs clopped through the streets. The sky had a pinkish tint from the recent snow.

A maid opened the door and Mrs Bloom bustled up behind her. Diamond studs glinted in her ears, and her freshly permed hair gave off waves of a chemical scent.

'I'm so glad you two made it! Shalom, shalom. Erna, that hat is adorable on you. Come in!'

As Erna and Klaus crossed the vestibule, they felt they hadn't so much entered the Blooms' living room as traveled to a foreign land. The smell of Mrs Bloom's hair was overpowered by sandalwood incense. A fire had been lit in the fireplace; with all the people crammed into the room, it was almost too humid. An actual stage, with a raised platform and a curtain, was set up in front of the bay window.

Gabriel stood in the corner, dressed in a toga Erna remembered from last year's Purim celebration. He gave them a little smile and wave.

'Gabe, darling,' said Mrs Bloom. 'I think we can begin now, if you'd like to sound the gong.'

He hurried off. In a few moments a satisfying crash reverberated through the room, and the guests went to find seats. Mrs Bloom walked up to the stage holding the arm of a man. Erna was surprised that the newcomer was dressed so informally, in khakis and an open-necked shirt. When he turned to face them, she guessed that he was in his early thirties. He had an olive complexion, with heavy-lidded eyes and thick eyebrows and lashes. His nose was broad, almost squashed-looking, but this somehow suited the exotic masculinity of his appearance. His lips were a dark shade of rose.

'Ladies and gentlemen!' called out Mrs Bloom. The dramatic cadence in her voice was only half-joking. 'Today, as many of you are already aware, we have an extra-special guest. A young man from West Philadelphia who's spent the last six months living in Palestine, taking photographs for *Life* magazine.' She patted the man's shoulder. 'Some of you already know him. His name is Melvin Katz. But of course I should introduce him as Yair Ben Ariel.'

One of the guests a few seats in front of Erna whispered to his wife: 'He changed his name after being there six months?'

Erna had to press a fingernail into the tip of her thumb to stop herself from laughing.

Melvin Katz, or Yair Ben Ariel, had heard the man, too. But he didn't seem embarrassed. He answered in a calm, sonorous voice that reminded Erna of a radio announcer's. 'Actually, I changed my name after being in Palestine for just three weeks. I guess it might seem excessive. But I was so moved by the experience that I had to acknowledge it somehow. I hope that after you see my photographs, you'll all be able to understand, even just a little, what a transformative effect the Holy Land can have on people.'

He nodded at Gabriel, who turned off the lights and dashed up to the side of the stage. The curtains pulled to either side, revealing a white screen.

'Today I want to show you a new breed of Jew,' Yair Ben Ariel said. 'The Jew of the Holy Land. The *sabra*. Does anyone know what a sabra is?'

The slide projector shuffled and an image appeared on the screen. Erna wondered what it was. Some kind of cactus?

He smiled. 'A sabra is a fruit. A prickly pear, to be exact. The native Jews of Palestine call themselves sabras because they're hard

by Rebecca Tyng Kantor

and tough on the outside, but sweet and sensitive on the inside.'

None of them had ever seen photographs like these. They had never seen Jews like these. These Jews weren't starving children in ghetto streets, looking at the camera with large eyes, or bearded Hasids bent over scrolls. They were young men and women in fields, lean and muscular from physical work.

A couple striding through the desert; the man had a scythe slung over his shoulder, and a Star of David pendant swinging against his chest. The woman was nearly as tall as he. Curls of hair sprung through the kerchief tied around her head.

Teenagers grouped around a campfire. All of them wore loose white shirts and shorts that set off their slim, tanned limbs. A girl strummed a guitar. Some of the others held hands. How different from Erna's experience at that age, newly arrived from Germany, her poor English making her shy and self-conscious with her classmates.

A line of Palestinian Jews in the British Army. Their caps threw clean shadows over their faces. In the distance, there were palm trees and the prickly pear plants. And the ruined building – Yair pointed to it – that was Masada, the ancient fortress where Jewish forces had committed mass suicide rather than be captured by the Roman soldiers.

Erna forgot that she was a small person whose skin burned red in the sun. Her body pulsed with energy. These were her people, the Jews of the desert, the natives of the Holy Land.

Yair clicked the slide projector. The screen went blank.

'Thank you very much,' he said. 'Gabe, would you turn on the lights? Thanks.'

The guests clapped. They turned to each other, smiling, as if they'd just witnessed some spectacle too breathtaking to describe in words.

Erna looked at Klaus.

'Wow,' he mouthed.

Mrs Bloom came up behind the two of them. 'Darlings, I must introduce you to Melvin. I mean, Yair. I've been going on and on about you two and now he's dying to meet you.'

She took them each by the elbow and steered them through the crowd. Yair Ben Ariel stood by the table of refreshments. Erna was struck again by his good looks. He could easily have been a sabra himself.

Yair surprised Erna by turning to her rather than to Klaus. 'Didn't you just have a show at the MacDuff gallery?'

'Oh – well, yes! I did.'

'I was there a few weeks ago and saw it. Your work is incredible. And you're studying at the Pennsylvania Academy of Fine Arts, right? I have some friends who went there, too.'

Mrs Bloom gave Erna's elbow a final squeeze and then let go. 'I'll leave you all to your artists' talk!'

In fact, after congratulating Yair on his photographs and lecture, Erna and Klaus couldn't think of a thing to say. Klaus gestured to the remnants of marinated lamb on his plate. 'Is this, uh, a food from Palestine?'

Yair nodded. 'The Jews there eat completely differently from us. Almost like Arabs. You wouldn't believe it, but the whole time I was on the kibbutz I was just dying for a roast beef sandwich.' He paused. 'Actually, would you two like to go have some dinner?'

'Sure! I mean, it sounds good to me,' said Klaus. 'Ernachen?'

'All right.'

Yair had a favorite deli in mind. He thought it was a few blocks away, but it ended up taking them nearly half an hour to walk there.

'I'm glad this place is still here!' he said when they arrived, as if he'd been gone six years instead of six months.

They slid into a booth and took off their coats. Erna now recognized Yair's white, open-necked shirt – it was the same outfit the men in his photographs wore.

'Very appropriate attire,' she said, smiling.

'Oh, ha! This.' He looked down at himself. 'This was actually Mrs. Bloom's idea. I guess she likes these dramatic effects. Did you see her poor kid, wearing that toga, or whatever it was –'

They laughed. But still the thought entered Erna's head: *Mrs Bloom might have asked you to wear those clothes, but she didn't force you to change your name after being in Israel for three weeks.*

by Rebecca Tyng Kantor

Erna tried her sandwich. The roast beef was tough. It was difficult to take a ladylike bite without pulling the whole thing apart.

'So, do you think you'll ever go back to Palestine?' Klaus asked Yair.

'Actually, that's part of the reason why I wanted to talk to you two. The Blooms are funding me to go back there in just a few months. What I'd like to do is to bring other artists with me. Painters, sculptors, maybe more photographers. The thing is, immigrants like our parents are so concerned with being American that they'd like to forget that they're Jewish. They forget that their heritage is something to be proud of. Sure, they help our efforts in Palestine in a practical way. If they hear that people are being killed, they'll donate to a relief fund. They tell themselves: we're helping these people because we're all human. It's our duty to help those in need. But why not help your fellow Jews because you're proud of being Jewish? Why not support Zionism because of the beauty of the idea? We have farmers in Palestine already, we're cultivating the land and all that. Still, we're not showing other people why these efforts are so important. So my idea is to start a whole community – maybe a kibbutz – of artists. Artists who will portray the Jews in the Holy Land for the rest of the world. In Palestine, we're rediscovering ourselves as farmers and soldiers. Why not as artists, too?' He swirled the dregs of his coffee and clinked the cup back into its saucer. 'I mean, maybe you don't consider photography an art …'

'No, no,' Klaus and Erna murmured. 'We do.'

'I just hope that in the future … that more people will feel the same way you do.'

'If they saw yours –' Klaus leaned forward and blushed.

'They're really good,' Erna said. 'Your photographs.'

Yair seemed to have forgotten about her before, but now he turned to her and smiled. 'Thanks.'

He took two framed photographs from his briefcase and presented them to Klaus and Erna. They were copies of a picture from the slide show – the Zionist flag surrounded by smiling young men.

'So,' Yair said as they left the deli. 'Will you think about it?'

'What?' Erna asked.

'Coming to Palestine with me.'

'Oh ...' said Klaus. He looked around at the cold street, the patches of slush under the trees on the edge of the sidewalk. The bells of St Peter's began to chime the aborted melody that signaled the half-hour. Yair would have done better to ask them while they were still in the warmth of the deli, Erna thought, the food evoking nostalgia for the quaint Jewish childhood neither of them had really had. She could guess what Klaus was thinking. Palestine was a beautiful idea. But to actually go there?

....

Rebecca Tyng Kantor studied English with a concentration in creative writing at the University of Pennsylvania. She has written for various publications, including *The Pennsylvania Gazette*, *Peregrine*, and *Artblog*. In 2010-11, she was awarded a Fulbright scholarship to do research for a novel. She is the recipient of the 2011 Seth Donaldson Memorial Bursary.

by Rebecca Tyng Kantor

Kate Macrae

The Fish Ladder
An excerpt from a book combining fiction, travelogue and memoir

SPEY

A buzzard perched on the 'welcome' sign in the small Highland town of Grantown on Spey. Its one visible eye peered into my own, a bright pulse of contact as I drove past. I had made a reservation at the same hotel where our family used to holiday each summer, although it was decades since I had last been here. After meandering up and down the side roads running parallel to the main street I eventually found the Springfield Lodge Hotel. The gravel drive had given way to a car park, and the croquet lawn at the back had disappeared beneath new houses. But for the most part the house was familiar and when I walked through the double doors I was greeted by the same heavy walnut writing desk where a Victorian display case still housed a collection of hand-tied fishing flies that shimmered, soft as tinsel, over their hooks. I hurriedly lifted my hands from the glass when I realised that a woman was staring at me.

'Can I help you?' She was the receptionist.

'Yes, thank you, I have a reservation for tonight. Katharine Thomson.' She peered at the computer screen in front of her.

'Is everything all right?'

'I think so,' she said, 'I have you down for tonight and for two days hence but not tomorrow. Is that right?'

'Yes,' I said, 'I plan to follow the Dunbeath Water from the sea to its source. I will be spending tomorrow night on the hills.'

'The hills?' she said, 'my goodness. Do you want me to hold the room for you? It's forecast rain!'

'No.' I said, 'Thank you. Can you do breakfast for me at seven, though?'

'We can. Good luck with it if I don't see you in the morning. Callum will take your bag to your room.' I couldn't see anyone who might have been Callum so I picked up my holdall and made for the stairs.

The hotel had seemed vast in my recollection but was in fact no more than two floors of rather grand rooms which our extended family of grandparents, parents, aunts, uncles and cousins, together with me and my brother, must pretty well have filled. And then there was Mr Kenneth Yields, a gentleman fisherman who always took his holiday at the same time as us. Mr Yields had helped me land my first brown trout in the River Spey, when I was eight, and the kitchen staff had cooked it for breakfast.

After finding my room I decided to walk to the river. A sign directed me through a wood of green-black firs. The bilberries had gone, the blackberries were not yet ripe. Gold lichen-tufted boulders stained tea-coloured by the peat. Toadstools pushed through moss. The forest scent was pungent; a soft sweet churchy resin over mushroom over mulch. A whisper passed through the trees, its soughing breath blowing a confetti of falling leaves. They were the first messengers of a change in air pressure, the front that I had remained ahead of, yet had followed me all day long.

My memory of the river was that it was black and smooth, travelling between green banks, the fish clearing the water in deep pools below the bridge. But as I came out of the woods I was greeted by a swollen, opaque, drowning river, matted with daisy-filled weeds, an Ophelia river that heaved against mudded banks. I tried to find the place where I had caught my first trout. Being seven years younger than my brother I was often left behind when he and my cousins went on expeditions. Sometimes Mr Yields would take me fishing. I recalled, at the end of one afternoon, my aunt making her way towards the water's edge in her PVC cream mac, approaching warily, yet sassily, in inappropriate heels, her smile a vermillion streak, her unnecessary sunglasses glinting in the weak sun. For the very first time it struck me that this occurrence might have been unusual, my

by Kate Macrae

aunt coming down to the river, and she and Mr Yields wandering off, leaving me to oversee the rods. *Now you watch the lines ... Keep your eye on the float ...* and then they would come back a while later. I remembered sheltering from the rain in a wooden fisherman's hut, alone. Alone! Spots of rain had dropped through the water's surface, causing circles as big as my head. I had made a prop from a forked twig, to support my fishing rod, and devoted myself to carving my initials into the doorjamb of the hut with a penknife.

I turned the memory, questioned it, for it seemed unlikely. I was chilly, the rain was coming fast behind the wind, which was rising, so I left the water, and hurried back through the skittering forest.

By the time I got back to the hotel I was soaked. I walked up the wax-polished staircase, feeling the burnt dark caramel of oak, its textured grain beneath my wet hand, and at a right-angled bend met another splintered recollection, bright and translucent as film. I had a sudden clear image of myself crouching on this first floor landing, my hair unkempt, the laces of my damp pumps dirty as worms, and watching in fascination through the rails while my uncle, who was a jazz musician and had the floppy hair and angular cheekbones of Chet Baker, raised one hand in warning, and argued vehemently across the stairwell – presumably in full hearing of everyone – with the waistcoated and tweedy figure of Mr Yields, who blinked, and polished his spectacles, but nonetheless stood his ground. *I don't need you to teach my wife how to fish!*

I shivered as I turned the key in the door to my room. I walked straight through to the bathroom and ran the taps on an enormous roll-top bath. An hour later I pulled on a pair of jeans and a sweater. I took a book from my holdall, Neil Gunn's *The Highland River*, as the book described, in the form of a novel, the journey that I hoped to make the following day.

A table had been set for me in the dining room, silver service, a crisp white damask tablecloth, but with the exception of the shopkeeper and the lady on reception I had been alone all day. I craved the sudden intimacy of the bar. There was a deep Knole leather sofa, next to an oak coffee table, in front of the fire, so I sank into this and ordered a venison salad. I watched the young barman talking to a German couple about whisky. I wondered if he was the absent Callum who the receptionist had referred to earlier, the one who had failed to collect my bag. The German couple wanted to know if a single malt whisky was better than a blend, and if age was an indication of quality. He answered them knowledgeably, yet evenly, exhibiting no personal preference, nor implying any hint of stigma or qualitative judgement, so that while being very well informed about whisky – in the abstract – they did not seem any the wiser, with regard to making a decision, by the time he had finished.

I opened the *The Highland River*, and immersed myself in the opening chapter. Gunn described how a young boy was sent by his mother to fetch water from the well-pool close by the river-mouth. There he disturbed a great cock-salmon, and he wrestled with it, and brought it to land. The fine hairs stood up on my forearm when reading the account: 'If the pool be just deep enough a salmon will pass between swimming human legs rather than be driven forth, and in this restless fashion will ultimately tire out its enemies.'[1] I was surprised, when I glanced up, to find the barman removing my plate and asking me if I wanted anything else. He was standing in the space between me and the coffee table. Our feet almost touching. As if in response to my unspoken discomfiture, he glanced behind him and down at the table, which was heavy, and pressed into the backs of his calves. He shrugged, creating an impression of a vague but deliberate insolence. Well, surely it would have been a little more orthodox to lean across from the side to clear the table? I put down the book.

'I'd like whisky,' I said, 'but I'll come and see what you have,' and I eased past him and walked over to the bar. He was attentive, professional. As before, he gave nothing away. He was between twenty and twenty-three. I made my selection, Glenfarclas, large, no ice but he had several bottles of various ages, and I allowed him to guide me through this second stage. Another young man appeared. The two of them exchanged a few words. The second man was offering to make up my order, and I understood that the shift had changed. My

by Kate Macrae

barman placed the heavy tumbler on a tray, accompanied by a jug of water. I slipped down from the bar stool in order to move back to my seat by the fire, but in that moment a couple from the dining room entered. He and I watched as they sat down on the sofa, filling it. The tray was suspended between us, he looked from it to me, and his eyes darkened, a momentary flaring of the pupil, as he said,

'Would you like me to bring this to your room?'

Stunned, I focused on the button that secured his regulation white shirt, the top button remaining unfastened. The skin of his throat was pale and this, combined with the white of the cotton and the fairness of his hair, gave him a slightly studious look, but he exuded a butterscotch warmth. I was reminded of a comment made by one of H G Wells's lovers, when asked about his success with women: *his skin smelled of honey*. The shirt seemed tight across his shoulders, which were wide, and arched as taut as a bow. His waist was narrow, he was probably a climber, or perhaps a rower, the deltoid muscles pulling a ruck across the line of his shirt, the hand that held the whisky, strong. The distance between us expanded, and then shrank, very quickly, back to nothing. I was aware of the planes of his body that were facing mine, and sensed a movement as silent, yet frenetic, as Brownian motion, as a thousand tiny signals coursed between us.

I lifted my eyes and met his look, causeway to an unknown land. Crowded into that handful of seconds was the aching realisation that beauty follows a law of diminishing return. I was aware of the exquisitely finite nature of the moment. But regardless of the fact that I am a married woman, regardless of the fact that I have a child, the truth was that I did not want to wake up and see this young man's head on my pillow, to have to step over his discarded shoes, or even speak with him.

'I'll take the whisky here,' I said, 'thank you,' and as my hand took the glass the diamonds that formed my wedding ring glittered under the halogen lights of the bar. But I kept his gaze, was held in it, and for those few brief moments I felt all the promise and wonderment implied there, the feckless possibility of hidden joy, urgent and unfettered, ephemeral as the smell of hot bread; until quite suddenly he coloured, a deep flush rising from his collar, creeping towards his cheekbones, and he dipped his head, and looked away.

....

[1] Thanks to the estate of Neil M Gunn for permission to quote this line.

Kate Macrae trained as a film editor and script editor with the BBC and was Eddie Izzard's stylist. She began writing four years ago her own hybrid of fiction, travelogue and memoir.

by Kate Macrae

Peter Matthews

Palegate House
An extract from a novel

The phone goes in the middle of the night. Matthew stumbles out of bed. His mind is sleep-fogged; it is like being in an aquarium; he cannot tell what is inside of the watery unreality and what is out. An aquarium? The image seems to come from the dream from which he has not fully woken.

'Matthew.'

'Shamil? Do you know what time it is?'

'Yes, I know. They wouldn't let me call before.'

'Who wouldn't?'

'There is a bag at my house. You should bring it to me.'

'What are you talking about? Where are you?'

'*Militsia*,' Shamil says. 'The police. They will move me again, but they don't say where. The bag is important, I need you to bring it.'

The trains are delayed. In front of the departures board, people slump on the grubby floor or perch on their luggage or huddle near the station's entrance and let out low groans as one train after another is cancelled or postponed. Outside, a line of transport police stands at the edge of the crowd, looking bored and puffing their cheeks against the cold. A wire-haired woman walks away from the line but turns back, her right hand clawing its way into a leather glove. Her voice rises. People turn their heads to watch.

'I don't care,' the woman says. 'I paid for a seat and I want a seat.'

Matthew approaches a uniformed woman nearby. 'Is the Oxford train running?'

'Platform thirteen,' says the officer, not looking at him.

'Where can I buy a ticket?'

She meets his eye.

'I wouldn't worry about it. Everything's late. Just get on the next one, as long as you don't mind standing.'

On the train, too, people cram on the floor. Matthew waits by the doors. When the train sets off, he leans against them with Shamil's drawstring bag wedged behind him. Through the facing window, fields swim past blue with snow, outlines of leafless trees are black against the dark horizon, the reflected spectre of himself looms over it all.

Clink's Bed and Breakfast is not far from the station, one of a row of narrow terraced houses that muddle up a hill. Matthew finds number thirty-three halfway along. It has a slightly degraded aspect: peeling paint, the flanking buildings smothering in on both sides. The front door is unlocked. It opens to a hallway with stripped floorboards and bare walls. At the bottom of the stairs, a bald man is asleep behind a desk. His hairy forearms stick out in front of him. Matthew clears his throat and, when the man doesn't wake, he touches his hand. The man looks up with a start, blinking to unstick his red-rimmed eyes.

'Is this Clink's?'

'Clint's,' the man says. 'You're late.'

'The trains.' Matthew hesitates. 'Is there any chance of food?'

'Bed and breakfast.' The man brings out a key from under the desk; one of the numbers on the metal tag is faded, it reads *0*. 'Up the stairs and on the left.'

Room no.10 of Clink's, or Clint's, has mustard wallpaper and a single iron frame bed that takes up enough space for Matthew to wonder how it got through the door. A catch prevents the window from opening more than a couple of inches. On the wall, an oil painting clumsily depicts the room itself.

In the bathroom, down the hall, a handwritten sign is Blu-tacked to the inside door: *Don't occupy for more than 30 mins. No couples in the bathroom at the same time. No pissing in the sink.* Matthew rinses out and fills the tub. Climbing into the steaming water, his feet sting

by Peter Matthews

and flower red. He soaks until the heat is spent, then turns the hot tap again. Past four in the morning, he wakes in a tank of wet cold.

Back in room 10, in the dark pre-dawn, Matthew unpacks Shamil's bag piece by piece: bright blue jeans recently ironed, a pink polo shirt. Matthew is no longer accustomed to seeing Shamil in clothes like these, he is more used to the chequered trousers and grubby white top the kitchen staff wear. Shamil's innovation: the work clothes. Who will do all that now, Matthew thinks? Who will pick up on all those things that Matthew does not see or sees and does nothing about?

Just as he is ready to return the clothes to the bag, Matthew sees the dirty green of a £5 note sprouting past a sock. He pushes the clothes aside: a bird's nest of old notes mat the bottom of the bag. He tips the money onto the bed and counts it – just over £300. Matthew goes to his jacket, takes out the envelope containing a further £200, and places it with the rest.

A clear, cold midday. Snow hunches at the sides of the road. The wind whistles, pauses for breath, whistles again. Ahead of Matthew is a woman wearing a long, grey coat. Each turn she makes through the icy streets, he makes too. Eventually, she sits down at a bus stop. Matthew approaches her. She is his age. She wears her neat white hair pinned back. Her skin is pale and ashy, frost-tightened to her skull.

'Excuse me,' he says. 'I'm looking for the bus to the detention centre.'

The woman does not answer but indicates past him with her eyes. The puffing vehicle lumbers up.

They are the only people to alight at Palegate House. On the far side of the road, snow-covered fields gape into the distance, ploughed black earth shows through here and there: fillings in massive howling mouths. This side is an iron fence. Behind the fence, a tarmac drive stretches up the hill to a series of toy-box structures.

'Where do we go now?' Matthew asks the woman.

She turns to him impassively. 'We have to wait for the driver.' As the bus heaves off, she regards him for what seems like the first time. 'Are you visiting your son?'

'No,' he says. 'I'm British.' *I'm British.* Meaning: *I am not one of them. A son of mine would not end up in a place like this.* It feels like a betrayal. He repeats himself: 'not my son. I'm visiting a friend.'

Down the road, gates open to allow a van out. It rounds the corner and pulls up beside them.

'What's your name?' Matthew asks, as they squash inside.

'Beatrice,' the woman says.

When they search the sports bag, they remove the money and place it under a counter. 'This needs to be processed with the detainee present. We'll give you a receipt.'

Spears of dusty light pierce the visiting room. From opposite walls, two guards face each other. They are both young: late teens or early twenties. Younger than Matthew's son, younger than his daughter, younger than Shamil. One boy catches the other's eye. They smirk.

A heavy door opens and Shamil is led out. He squints against the light. As he sits down opposite, Matthew notices the greyed inside collar of his shirt.

'Don't you have a change of clothes?'

'Did you bring the bag?'

'Yes.'

'So I have one.'

'I brought the money, too. They wouldn't let me give it to you here, but I have the receipt.' Matthew slides the creased slip over to Shamil, points at the printed figure. 'Five hundred and five pounds. That's everything from your bag. I added some myself.'

Behind Matthew, the door opens. Beatrice enters and seats herself a few tables away. Shamil watches her.

'The money I had,' he says. 'I saved it from my wage. I never took anything more.'

'I know,' Matthew says.

'Who will manage the kitchen now?'

'I'm not sure.'

by Peter Matthews

'Like always.'

'What do you mean?'

'I don't know how the police found me. Maybe someone told them. Maybe it was my landlord, maybe my neighbour, maybe you. That's how it works, this country. If you didn't have this,' Shamil indicates around, to the room they are in, to the guards at the side of the room, 'where would you be? Just an island where it rains. An island of people unsure about everything. Your rules are why people want to come here. Thank you for the extra money, but you don't owe it to me. You don't owe anything to me.'

Shamil takes the bag and looks through the things Matthew has brought. Behind him, the heavy door opens and a handsome, long-limbed African man is led out into the room. He walks over to Beatrice. She takes one of his hands in both of hers, and kisses it.

'Do they treat you well?' Matthew asks.

One of the young guards comes to their table. 'Your time's up.'

It is getting dark when Matthew is driven back down the hill. Steel fences line the road. Floodlights, shining through the fences, cast orange nets about the ground. They pass a young man in uniform, smiling goofily as he walks a German shepherd down the side of the road.

Matthew has missed the bus. The van driver offers to take him back – he can sit in the reception and drink tea from the vending machine.

'No. Leave me here.'

'You sure?' asks the driver. 'It's freezing.'

'I don't want to be taken back.'

Matthew waits facing away from Palegate House. He wants not to hear the groan of the place; the accumulative groan made by doors locking, showers, cooking food, the buzz of electric light, men murmuring, awake and asleep. The wind swells and breaks, waving the tree-shades across the field. Before long, the bus stop, which is only a sign fixed to a pole at the side of the road, is lit up by headlights. Another visitor ferried from the centre. The door slides open, Beatrice steps out.

'Thank you very much,' she says to the driver.

'Stay in the car if it's warmer,' he says. 'I'm not busy.'

'That's all right. It'll be here any minute now. But thank you.'

How is it she can speak cheerfully with a man who will drive back up the hill, lock her friend in his room and turn off the lights? The van turns and drives away. Beatrice is looking at him. He has been staring.

'Do you have something to say?'

'Why did you thank him?'

'Thank who?'

'I don't know who he is to you, that man you were visiting. But whoever he is, it's enough to make you come to him here. Why do you thank his jailers?'

What would he say if someone levelled such an accusation at him? He would say nothing. He would fall silent. Beatrice, though, looks at him evenly.

'And what should I do?' she says. 'Rant and rave? There is a process, whatever you think of it. My behaviour to that man, polite or not, can't help Junior. If making a scene would help Junior, then put your mind at ease, I would do. And who are you to ask me that? What gives you the right?'

The bus arrives. She raises her voice to be heard over the howl and growl of the wind and the engine. It is a ridiculous scene; two old people shouting in a field. The doors hiss open and they step on board into waxen light.

....

Peter Matthews grew up in London. After completing his BA at the University of East Anglia he won the Malcolm Bradbury Award for the best creative writing dissertation 2009. He has worked in London and Moscow and has been published in *The Guardian*. He is currently working on a novel called *Enclosure*.

by Peter Matthews

Erin Meier

Darling

You're walking around the lake. It's a beautiful day. The sun is out, shining benevolently over the willow trees around the greenish flat water. A slight breeze rustles the golden-orange leaves that have blown over the path. The autumn air is cool and smoky.

Other walkers parade by with dogs or strollers or just a relaxed smile. You're happy to leave the cold concrete walls of the university behind. I can't blame you really, it looks like a cross between a prison and a sacrificial temple with the strange glistening ziggurats of the dorms looming over the bunker-like lecture halls.

A chill breeze winds around your neck like a python. You shiver and pull the zipper of your jacket up past your soft waist and your breasts. They compress under the slick black Gortex. Windproof and rainproof you amble on.

A yellow-jacket darts past, buzzing importantly. You nod at a fisherman who reclines on a small dock, his pole and other gear arrayed about him like a king at a feast. He turns away from your greeting, and the smile slips from your face. You push your hands into the pocket of your jacket and walk faster, staring at something farther off.

When you come to the fork in the trail, you pause. A woman passes you, her spaniel's tongue lolling from its pink mouth. As you step aside, I see you glance at the second path, the one that leads off into the forest.

My breath catches in anticipation. You don't disappoint me. Your gray eyes are alight with interest. Something sparkles, flashes just beyond the trees. You stride into the forest, taking a swig from your water bottle as the gloom settles over you.

I love the way your hair shines as you move, an undulating ribbon of gold. As I creep along behind you I remember the day that I came upon you. Your rosy-white skin gleaming in the sunlight. How you lay prostrate on that boulder, bare as a mussel pulled from its shell. High in the Cascade mountains, miles from any human habitation. Somehow you found my little valley and you made yourself at home. I didn't mind. I wanted to knead your flesh as a baker kneads bread. I wanted to pull you around me like a starfish on a rock. But you went back to the city.

You don't belong here. We don't belong in this flat landscape of strange pigeons and greasy ivy that twines round the trees in a slow death strangle. And because I'd followed you to the city, I followed you here as well.

You beat me, in your queer flying machine, my slippery darling. After weeks in the belly of that ship, stinking of rot and creosote, I finally disembarked. It took me some time, but I found your scent. And now that I've found you again I'm taking you home.

Home to the smell of moss, and pine, and salt. Mountains that seem to tumble into the sea. You have a secret longing for it. I can see it in the way you gaze forlornly at the stunted shrubs that pass for underbrush. You miss the deep tangle of the Hoh rainforest, the frantic swell of the Dungeness River, and the rock-strewn coastlines of your childhood.

You pass quite closely to me as you round the corner. I sniff at the air, and grow weak at your nearness. I press against the tree, the bark catches at my fur. You wander down the path. A bird erupts from the underbrush and you give a small shriek. I feel that shriek in every part of me.

But I am cautious, oh so very cautious. I haven't tracked you this long only to lose you again. You continue down the trail, disconcerted, chuckling at your foolishness. But I see the uneasiness in the way you shift the pack on your back. The way your eyes dart ahead, and then glance with relief at the boy who appears further down the trail. He has a dirty face and he's whistling. He kicks at a conker on the

by Erin Meier

ground, smiles when you greet him. I can hear your heartbeat, the muddled thump of it.

It isn't easy to keep my seven-foot frame concealed. My callused hands rest against the soil. I crouch just behind a beech hedge. I pull the stillness into me as the little boy troops past. His nose twitches. He's caught my scent. A sour odor of fungus, cedar and decaying kelp. It's very strong, and usually that's how we're found out, my kind. The smell. But they've never managed to catch one of us. We're good runners, and we're used to hiding. 'Move on little one,' I think.

The boy passes, and then there is no one. It's time. I can feel it. The forest is quiet, a bird calls. Your heart beats languidly, patters. You stand calmly in the twilight, gazing blankly into the distance. Slowly, oh so slowly I creep forward. My heart is pounding loudly now, so loudly I can barely hear your footsteps ahead. I'm ecstatic with anticipation. You are so close now. I gaze at the soft furze of blond hair on your pale forearm. I hold back until ...

You don't hear me until my arms are around you. I cradle you against my chest. My little one. My pale darling. Your screams rend my ears. I ignore them, I know it will only be moments until you recognize me. You've seen me before, I came to you as a little girl, remember?

I turn and wade into the shrubs, we'll be safe farther away from others. You've pulled an arm from my grip and you reach up. Expecting a caress, I'm shocked to feel my hair being pulled from the roots. You hold a clump of it in your hand. My fierce darling. I adjust you in my arms, clamping you against me. Your heartbeat is like a bird's. Your body robust and malleable.

Why should you continue to scream? And why when that jogger burst through the bushes, and began to beat me about the head with a metal water bottle, why did you cheer? You fell from my arms so swiftly.

But as you both kicked at me, my only thought became escape. Escape because the jogger, that awful Amazon, had sunk her nails into my male parts. And as I ran into the trees, I heard her babbling about apes and zoos, the ridiculous woman. But you know me my darling don't you? You know me? You know me!

I'll be at your window tonight. I know it wasn't your fault.

Erin Meier is a prose writer from the Olympic Peninsula, in the United States. She studied English and Theatre at the University of Washington, where she staged several of her own one-act farces. In recent years, she has switched from writing plays to prose fiction. Currently, she is writing a novel set in the Pacific Northwest during the late nineteenth century.

by Erin Meier

Anna Metcalfe

Thread
Excerpt from a story

They're here, she said.
    Yes, he replied. His voice was deep and cool.
Saba opened the door. Three men stood in the yard beside a truck. She nodded at them, they nodded back and she turned to face her husband to say goodbye. She did not cry as she'd thought she might. Instead, she felt herself getting smaller, or perhaps it was the room getting bigger: white-washed walls shooting up to the sky, the stone floor levelling out like spilt coffee. Mussa took her in his arms and she shrank further.
    Be careful, he said.
    He loaded his two small canvas bags onto the back of the truck and clambered in after them. She couldn't see how many others were inside. All she could see was the shudder of the grey tarpaulin as they pulled away.
    It was five thirty and the sun was almost up. Saba waited on the threshold. When the sound of the truck had faded into the early traffic, she closed the door. The skirt of her dress caught in the frame. When she stepped back into the room, she heard the fabric rip.
    Saba stooped and pulled gently at the white cotton until it came free. The tear was in the seam, a tangled split of about four inches. She walked across the room and slid the sewing box from under the bed. With shaking hands, she carried it to the table, spools of thread rattling against the thin wooden case. She sat down and hitched up her skirt to smooth the seam across the table's surface. With hands splayed over the fabric, she steadied herself, pressing into the table as though to absorb its solidity. She focused her eyes on the seam

and picked a needle from a pin cushion. She pulled white thread from a spool and, in one swift motion, fed it through the needle's eye. With a momentary surge of confidence, she began to sew and, in minutes, the rip was mended. But when she looked at her handiwork closely, Saba saw that the join was clumsy with most of the stitches misaligned. She sat with the seam pulled taut between her hands and did nothing.

She had hardly slept. In the night, she had touched Mussa's arm from time to time, to comfort him or herself, to see whether or not he was awake. He had remained still, breathing softly, though she sensed he was not asleep. Saba had learnt that stillness was his way of being calm.

They had been married a year. The first six months, Mussa spent in military service, working at the border, repairing rail tracks damaged during the war. When he returned – skin darker, hands rougher – he went back to his job at the university. When the education reforms were enforced, teachers and students protested. He was arrested. They kept him for two months. This time, he returned paler, thinner. After that he saw no future in Asmara.

Saba had seen him scared but never fraught; sad, but never inconsolable. He did things slowly and with purpose, as though his very movements protested the city's atmosphere of uncertainty and deceit. His steadiness gave him an air of permanence, of force. She pictured him, teeth and muscles clenched, holding his spine tall, as the truck skimmed the uneven earth towards the desert.

While Mussa was in prison, Saba had been disturbed more than once by men from the military who had come to search the room. They had not appeared to be looking for anything in particular. They took any money they found and, on one occasion, demanded food. They drank a bottle of wine she had kept, left over from her wedding day.

The things she considered important, Saba kept in a shallow metal tin, stowed under the sink beneath a pile of newspapers. She fetched it, now, and placed it on the table next to the sewing box, leaving papers scattered across the floor. She sat before the two open

by Anna Metcalfe

boxes: one on the left full of coloured threads, the other, on the right, an assortment of inked papers and occasional photographs.

The first poem she picked up was one she had performed on her father's birthday. It was six lines long and scribbled on an old receipt. Other poems in the tin were written on loose sheets of notepaper or the backs of advertisements snatched from café windows. Reading them over, she found that many of them were still committed to memory. She would get halfway through and lift her eyes from the page to find the words were still flowing. For the most part, they were occasion poems, made to order for family events. She placed these memorised works in a small pile at one end of the table and read on. There were some poems she no longer cared for and these, too, joined the pile. She picked through the pages one by one. By the time she had finished, all that remained were a handful of unlearnt stanzas, a photograph from her wedding and one of her family – both sets of grandparents, her mother and father, sisters, aunts, uncles and cousins, taken when she was five.

Saba took a jar of raw coffee beans into the yard. She stoked the fire, threw a fistful of beans into a heavy iron pan and placed it over the heat. She went back inside and bundled the unwanted papers into her arms. Sitting by the fire, waiting for the beans to roast, Saba fed poems to the flames. When the beans were ready, she ground them and boiled water. She brewed the coffee in a clay jebena while scraps of paper curled to ashes.

She poured coffee and went back into the room. The photographs she placed in a brown paper envelope and slid into the sewing box, beneath the pin cushion. She tore a couple of fresh sheets from a notebook and divided them into narrow strips. Onto these she copied the surviving poems in small, neat handwriting. She rolled each strip of paper into a miniature scroll and placed each scroll inside a spool of thread. She closed the empty tin and returned it to the space beneath the sink, stacking the newspapers on top. She threw the original poems in the fire. When the fire was no more than a few dull embers and the jebena was empty, Saba replaced the lid of the sewing box and slid it back under the bed.

Anna Metcalfe was born in Germany and grew up in Britain. She studied Literature and Translation at the University of York. She has worked in China and France. She is writing a collection of stories.

by Anna Metcalfe

Will Miles

Geminids
An extract from a short story

At the back door, Ian puts on boots, Toby his trainers – red canvas ones with blue stars and white caps. Ian almost says something about the frost, but he doesn't want to nag him – he's eighteen now.
'Should be a good one,' Ian says. 'No moon this year.'

2005. Back in Reading. Toby clutching a Tupperware box of Susan's Christmas brownies. A full moon, straight above their heads. Absolute write-off.

There's not so much as a fingernail clipping of moon tonight. It's a good year. This is a good year. Ian heads out first and it's metallic cold, as if pipes are threading up his sleeves, iron filings down his back. They cross the paving slabs and pass through the trees which divide the row of houses from the open countryside. Ian makes for the centre of the field, Toby crunching through the frost somewhere behind.
Ian sets his mug on the brim of a water trough, slabbed with thick ice. Toby steps beside him, then slurps noisily, as if he's using a straw.
Neck craned, Ian trains his eye to the Gemini oblong. It's like Chinese lettering or hieroglyphs. If you don't know the alphabet, you can't tell if you're reading a joke or a threat. Take Susan. She'd point up at the trapezium head of Draco, and wouldn't have a clue what it was. *Which one's that? Is that one of the zodiacs?* It was as if she wasn't really looking at it. She couldn't see the dragon's tail that bent and buckled round the pole star, Ursa Minor prodding into its arched form.

Toby slurps again.

'Chocolatey enough for you?' Ian asks.

'Yeah,' Toby says. He shivers. 'Thanks, Dad.'

The first meteor goes. The white of a spinning knife, grazing Orion's shoulder, threatening to slice the bow out his hand. Then it's dead in a second.

'See that one?' Ian says, scanning for more.

'It was good.'

They're two a minute. Well, 120-160 per hour, if you're there at the right time, and they are. They always are. 02:00-03:00 every December 14th.

The next is slower, a golf ball putted, then sinking into its hole.

Ian looks across. His son, breath steam-training out of him, takes another slurp, staring at the orange haze of the town in the west. He's got a ski-slope nose, a Susan nose. Ian's eyes though – not his words, Susan's. Can't see them now, of course, but a sort of browny-green.

2008. The first time Ian met Susan's boyfriend. Keith drove up in Susan's car at a service station outside Basingstoke to drop Toby off. They chatted over polystyrene cups of coffee. On the way home, Ian asked Toby (and he thinks he meant it seriously, not as a joke or a dig), if Keith was on TV. Toby laughed no. He looked like a presenter from one of those walking or history programmes called *Norman Walks* or *Big British Ruins*, one of those well-framed forty year olds who stride up hills in technical raincoats.

Two at once. Ian spots the first, his eye corners the other. One cuts the black void of the north sky, the other scissors the Milky Way tapestry, dies in the Dog.

'See those?' Ian says.

'Yeah, they're really good.'

1999. Gibbous moon, but low in the east, which is fine, really. Susan cross at Ian for getting their son up at that time. Toby red-mittened, Ian in stiff garden gloves. 'Do they mind, the others? Does

by Will Miles

the Dog mind having stars thrown at him?'

'No,' Ian said, 'no, the Dog doesn't mind. The twins are throwing bones for him.'

Something beeps. Briefly, Ian thinks car horn. Then he knows. The blue screen lights up his son's face. Ian didn't realise he'd brought it out. Toby paces a few steps away, the sound of the phone keys harsh in the quiet field. Twice since he's got here Ian's seen the name ringing on his mobile. Josh. Then Hannah. Neither was familiar. Or had there been a Josh at his school? Skinny lad, lots of acne, mum was a gardener. Maybe that was a Jake.

He hears low muttering. Toby's standing twenty feet away, looking downwards. Who takes/makes calls at – Ian lights up his watch – 02:18?

But it's not his business. He's watching a meteor dart towards Aldebaran. Taurus's eye, the red-white of watered-down Ribena.

Toby's missing uni. It's natural. Or home. He's bored of the countryside. Of course he's bored of it. Eighteen year olds hate the country. They're meant to. All his friends are near his mum and Keith's.

It's the longest they haven't seen each other for. After the split in 2007 they did pretty much every other weekend, except when Toby went on holiday with school for five days, to Paris or Rome or somewhere. But it was easy to pick things up after a few weeks. Not much had changed. His friends and haunts were all the same. But these uni terms are over two months.

Three days ago on the platform with stiff pats on the shoulder Ian tried not to say it but still, he'd shot up. He laughed, gone on any castle walks, Tobes? *That's not really Keith's thing.* Only kidding, Tobes. Ian felt stupid. It wasn't a dig. It wasn't meant to be a dig. He liked Keith. He started to wonder what else might be wrong, realised the absurdity of his Advent calendar purchase. What had he been thinking? Thank God he'd not put it in Toby's room.

He sees a meteor guillotine the coat hanger, the backward question mark, of the Lion's head.

Toby laughs into the phone, thirty feet away. Breathily. Out the nose, like when it's meant to be held back. A classroom laugh. Ian remembers himself younger than Toby doing that same laugh in English lessons.

Toby's got the phone to his ear. He starts muttering. What kind of muttering is that? Maybe Ian should ask about Hannah. Or even Josh. Maybe he'll do it tomorrow afternoon when they're full but the table's nicely littered with patties of bread sauce and pigs-in-blankets shiny with fat. They'll have lagers. Maybe two. He's never been tipsy with Toby but it'll be good. Leftovers at seven. Then they'll watch a murder mystery or something, and make smart-arse comments about the wooden acting or the stupid twists.

2006. Ian's last Christmas in Reading. He and Susan sitting in stony silence while the crime drama wound on, Toby plucking chocolates from a purple tin.

'Sorry, Dad,' Toby says, crunching back in the frost, dropping the phone in pyjama pocket, canvas shoes steeped in dew.
'Not to worry.'

They stare, expectant, into the black. Positioned just north of Castor, the fainter twin, is the radiant, the unmarked spot which is the apparent source of the Geminid meteors. They start wherever but they always travel away from this point. It's just a case of looking, then catching one and following it for its one- sometimes two-second lifespan.

Snick snick. Ian turns to see Toby twist his neck, put his mug on the grass, then push his coccyx with both hands, his arms stuck out in a two-handled jug. Crack.

Ian cricks his own neck. Bones snap like popcorn in a pan. He realises he's copying his son.

'Makes you ache a bit, looking up,' he says.

'Yeah,' Toby says, and snicks his neck again. 'I made my back stiff rowing, had to see a physio at uni.'

'Didn't say you were a rower.'

by Will Miles

'I only did it once.'

'You gonna keep it up?'

Toby picks up his mug. 'Maybe. I s'pose I could go again.'

'Good exercise rowing, I would've thought. Your uncle used to do it. He might still do. You'll probably see him some time over the hols. You should mention it to him.'

Ian hasn't received a card from Susan's brother yet. He's probably almost off their list. It's normally just *Dear Ian*, – pre-written message – *Anthony and Emma*, in Emma's squashed schoolgirl handwriting.

'There,' Toby says, pointing, but his hand's already going limp.

'Missed that. Good one?'

'Yeah. It was really quick. In the Chariot. The Charioteer. What's he called again?'

Auriga. Ian can read them side by side, the Latin names he learnt and the English names he first taught Toby with.

Aquila: eagle

Boötes: herdsman

Ian grabs his drink off the trough, sips the residual warmth. 'Got me thinking now.' Then he says it slowly as if he's just learnt it. 'Aw-ree-guh. That's the one. Yeah, that's it. Auriga.' He laughs. 'Old age.'

Toby does a nose laugh, all breathy. Must be his normal laugh now. It's not his secret one. He wasn't using a classroom laugh on the phone.

Another darts east, kicks the Crab.

'It's not too bad in Exeter either,' Toby says. 'For stars.'

'Shouldn't you be drinking?'

'But sometimes at night. 'Cause the campus isn't right in the city. I was showing my friend one of them. On the way back home. She didn't even know Orion.'

Ian nods, then sees, points, says *there*, all at once.

Almost straight out the radiant now, from twin to twin, as if they're kids playing ball. Castor throws. Pollux catches.

'That was a good one,' Toby says. He slurps.

'You're right, Tobes. Yeah, that was a good one.' Ian lights his watch again. 02:24.

Geminids

'They're always best around half past.'
'You know what we should've done?' Toby says.
'What's that?'
'Mulled wine.'
'Yeah, I thought about putting some on. I've got some for tomorrow though. I thought after lunch.'

Ian crosses lager off the list in his head and for the fourth time that night, or second time that morning, he finds himself mentally scaling down the Christmas cooking schedule in his Home Ec book, as he calls it.

Then the brightest one yet, going from faint to burning-bright to faint again.

Now Toby's looking at the horizon, at a pylon rising like a ship's mast. He's bored. He's definitely bored. The best ones have been. Of course he's bored. He wants to go back to bed, back to Reading.

Two more meteors spark outwards from the Twins.

Neither says anything. Toby's not enjoying himself. Of course. Ian feels stupid and bright red, and embarrassed heat's prickling his skin like a rash. He's made his son get up at two in the morning to stand in a frosty field.

'There's another good one,' Toby says. He's keen again. That was definitely keenness.

1976. Ian was 16. At his nan's, as they were every Sunday, his mum and dad and sister. Just before Easter. 'I know what Ian's after,' his nan said with her big-bad-wolf grin. 'Look at that smirk.' And she brought out of the cupboard under the stairs a box of hollowed eggs and paintbrushes and poster paints – always blue, pink and yellow. His sister left to see her new boyfriend, her parents said they'd pick Ian up in the evening.

They watch meteors in silence.

1977. 'What the fuck are they?' one of his friends laughed, looking at the eggs on the mantelpiece. 'My sister does them every year,' Ian said. And he bounced the butt of his lager bottle on each shell. Six Humpty Dumpties.

Will Miles was born in Dorset in 1989. He graduated with first class honours in English at the University of Bristol where he was editor of the student newspaper. He is currently writing his first novel.

by Will Miles

Claire Powell

The Girls
An extract from a short story

I found them in her bedroom: two black leather legs with a pale chiffon blouse laid out on top of the perfectly spread duvet – an invisible woman sleeping. I backed quietly out of the room as though I didn't want to disturb, closed the door gently behind me and stood on the landing, unsure of what I'd seen.

Downstairs, I leant with folded arms against the kitchen door frame, watched as she unloaded the dishwasher. I asked, 'What's with the outfit?'

She stopped what she was doing, looked down at her top. 'What, this?'

'No. The one on your bed.'

'Oh, that,' she said, and she carried on unloading, piling plates into the cupboard. 'D'you like it? Thinking of wearing it Friday for Michelle's birthday.'

'They're leather,' I told her, as if she'd not yet noticed. '*Leather* trousers.'

'They're comfy,' she shrugged. 'They're a nice fit. Stretchy.'

'Mum,' I said. 'They're for young people.'

'I am a young person. Young at heart,' and she reached for her pack of menthols, opened the back door. 'Besides,' she said, lighting up, 'what you doing in my bedroom anyway? Don't be nosy.'

On Friday, after work, I drove to her house. I told her I needed to borrow her blender. Really I wanted to check whether she was actually wearing the outfit. During the day – while I made cups of tea, signed parcels from couriers, answered the telephone in my telephone voice – I realised I'd not seen my mum on a night out for some time. Were leather trousers just the start of it? Did she wear mini-skirts to The Queen's Head? Hot-pants to the cinema?

She answered the door in bare feet, toenails the colour of armbands. Her hands were behind her neck trying to do up the catch on her necklace. I helped her with it, stood behind her in the mirror. She was wearing the outfit. It looked different filled in, filled up, 3D. The blouse was light and loose and covered her bum, but the leather trousers – the leather leggings – were tight, shiny, *leathery*.

She asked, 'You like?' and she twirled for me, tip-toes.

'Who you going out with?'

'Just the girls.'

'The *girls*?' I mocked, but she ignored me.

'Blender's there.'

The blender was sat on the stairs, black cord coiled round it, waiting to be collected. I picked it up.

'Where you going?'

She was walking between the front room and the kitchen looking for something.

'West End,' she said. 'You not out tonight?'

'Nah,' I said, hugging the blender to my belly. 'I'm cooking for Steve.'

This wasn't true. We were getting kebabs. Steve was picking them up on his way home from work.

'That'll be nice,' my mum said, and she read an old receipt from her handbag, chucked it in the bin.

I followed her into the kitchen. She sat down, pulled a pair of black ankle boots over her feet.

'Don't fancy a drink do you?' I was looking in her fridge.

'Don't have time,' she said, and her phone vibrated. 'That'll be the cab. Give us a kiss.'

I couldn't sleep. I lay awake and pictured my mum at a Wetherspoon's, All Bar One, Tiger Tiger. I felt hot, sweaty. I fidgeted next to Steve's sleeping body – legs under the cover, legs over the cover; hands under the pillow, hands on top of the pillow.

I wanted to drive up there and collect her. Wait for her outside like a parent at a disco leant against the car door, smoking a cigarette. I wanted to make sure that when my mum left she saw me, her daughter – not a man pretending to be a cab driver, a foreign accent asking, 'Taxi darling? Taxi darling?'

I pictured her downing shots at the bar. Throwing back miniature glasses of tequila, sambuca. I pictured her on the dance floor, dancing not as she did at my auntie's wedding – when she took each of her nieces one by one, twirled them around the hall of the sports club – but in a grimy, grinding way, backing up into the denim crotch of a man reeking of aftershave.

I wanted to collect her, to put her in the back where the seat was soft – not leather interior like some of those cabs. Leather thighs squeaking against leather seat. I wanted to take her home, turn up the radio, listen to Phil Collins, Marvin Gaye, the music only crackling as we drove back through the darkness of the Blackwall tunnel.

I phoned her the next morning. She didn't pick up. I tried four times then switched off my phone, buried it under my pillow. I watched morning telly, volume louder than usual. I sat on the settee one leg crossed over the other, foot in furry slipper shaking in the air. I chewed the skin around my nails, picked tiny flecks of chipped pink varnish off the tip of my tongue. I made Steve a bacon sandwich but couldn't eat my own. I ran a bath, lay back, ears under the water so all I could hear was my heavy breathing and the plop-plop-plop of the tap still dripping. I washed my hair, scrubbed it into a mango lather, eyes closed, trying to change my thoughts with my fingertips, to conjure other things: things to do and things to buy.

When I got out I rubbed myself dry and tipped my head upside down to tie a towel turban round it. As I did this a memory came back – as though it'd fallen from the back of my head to the front. I pictured the time when I was seven or eight and had slipped into a splits stepping out of the bath, my bird-like legs in an upside down V over the edge of the tub. I'd screamed. My mum came running in, her hair in a scruffy ponytail, still holding a pair of my dad's socks she'd been sorting from the wash. She swooped me up in her arms, carried me into her bedroom then lay me down on her bed, placed a cold flannel between my legs, like a large purple sanitary towel.

I thought of calling someone. *Police, please. I want to report a missing person. My mum. 5' 4", short brown hair, age 48. Wearing black leather trousers at last sighting.* I took my phone and switched it back on. I tried her again. She answered.

'I'm about to do Zumba,' she said, sounding already out of breath.

I felt relieved at first, my stomach muscles relaxed. Then I asked, 'Who with?'

'Couple of the girls. Just Linda and her mate Vicky.'

'I thought you only did aqua aerobics. Since when've you started doing Zumba?'

'Since a while now,' she said. 'It's just a bit of fun.'

I had an idea: a bit of fun. I searched on Google for spa retreats. I typed the words: Mum Daughter Spa Retreat. It came back with 3,680,000 results. I wondered why I'd never thought of this before. The past three years I'd only ever been on holiday with Steve. I wondered when my mum last went on holiday. Was it with me and Dad all those years ago? I wanted to treat her, relax with her, talk to her, confide in her …

'I'm going to Marbella,' she said, when I phoned and asked what she was doing June 18th. 'But I'm free the weekend after.'

'Marbella?' I said. 'I didn't know you were going to Marbella. Why you going there?'

'It's a hen do. Lorraine from work's getting married.'

'A *hen* do? Don't tell me you're doing the normal stuff.'

She laughed. 'What normal stuff? Plastic willies and Chippendales? Hope we are!'

'Don't be disgusting Mum.'

'Oh come on! Can't a girl have a bit of fun?'

'You're not a girl.'

'Why you getting upset?' she said. 'I'm not hurting no one, am I?'

'But this isn't you. You don't wear leather trousers.'
'Course it's me, don't be ridiculous.'
'Fine. Just don't come crying to me if something happens to you.'
'Stop it,' she said. 'Stop acting like a baby.'

I put the phone down, threw it across my bedroom so it thumped into the mound of dirty washing in the corner.

Steve poked his head round the door, asked, 'What's wrong with you?'

I told him – 'Nothing.'

Steve went to the pub and I put on my tracksuit – faded blue cotton, threadbare on the bum. I curled up as small as I could under the covers, sucked my thumb.

I searched for my mum on Facebook and found her. We had three friends in common – my cousins from Australia who we hardly even knew. Why hadn't she requested me as a friend?

I clicked on her profile picture. It was an old photo. The colour was different – more faded, almost yellow. She must've scanned it in. In my office it was against company policy to use the scanner for personal reasons. My mum was a receptionist too, but she worked in a primary school. I wondered if her office allowed personal scanning, or if she had a friend who had one, or if she'd bought a scanner herself. I didn't even think she owned a computer.

The photo was taken at the seaside – she was sat down on pebbles, there was a pier in the background. Margate? Brighton? Southend-on-Sea? I wondered if it was taken before or after me. She had long straight hair and a blunt fringe, was smiling at the camera holding a 99 ice-cream. Steve looked at the screen over my shoulder, pulled on my ponytail, said 'Doppelgänger.'

I wasn't allowed to look at her wall. It said she only shares some information publicly. It said if you know her add her as a friend. I lingered the cursor over the friend request button, then I clicked back to my own profile. My picture was of Steve and me smiling, his arm around me at the pub, fruit machine twinkling behind us. I wondered if she'd found me; wondered if she'd even looked.

The Girls

I had to return the blender. It'd been a week, I'd ignored her texts. Steve suggested I take a bunch of flowers, said my mum had a hard enough time with my dad, didn't need aggro from me. I took a box of chocolates – Assorted Pralines from the garage.

'What you like?' she said, when she opened the door.

'Sorry,' I said. My eyes and armpits stung.

She laughed and brought me to her, but I had a blender in one hand and chocolates in the other, so my arms just fell at my side and she held me, rubbed my back.

'Come through. Come say hello to my friends.'

I heard voices, saw two women standing in the kitchen holding glasses of wine, the back door open.

'Just need the loo,' I said, and I passed her the chocolates.

I took the stairs two at a time, locked the bathroom door behind me. I waited. I felt something hot rising in my chest. I didn't want to meet Vicky or Linda or Lorraine. I looked in the mirror above the sink. The mirror was also a cabinet. I opened the latch on it gently, heart beating, afraid of what I'd find. Condoms? Diaphragm? Sex toys? Maybe they'd had an Ann Summers party, bought lube or handcuffs, neon pink dildos.

I found a tub of anti-ageing cream, a tube of unopened toothpaste and five miniature perfumes, all lined up neatly.

The doorbell rang. It made me jump. I closed the cabinet quickly, surprised to see my face again. I wondered if I could just leave, slip out the front door without anyone noticing. I sat down on the lid of the toilet, held the blender on my lap like a small child.

Claire Powell was born in Greenwich. Her stories have appeared in *Station Magazine, Volume* and *Untitled Books*. In 2011 she received the Malcolm Bradbury Bursary Prize. She is currently working on a novel.

by Claire Powell

Natasha Pulley

The Watchmaker of Filigree Street

This is the first chapter of a novel about a watchmaker who remembers the future. The year is 1883, the beginning of an Irish bombing campaign in London that became known as the Dynamite War. Working as a telegraphist at the Home Office, Thaniel Steepleton is in the middle of it all, and soon, his life will depend on an inexplicable gift from a man he has never met.

The Home Office telegraphy department always smelled of tea. It was a mystery to all four operators. Or rather, three thought it was a mystery, and one pretended that it was. Nathaniel Steepleton kept a packet of Lipton's at the very back of his desk drawer, tucked into his own cup. He felt guilty for not sharing, but although tea was cheap, tea for four people every day was not.

It was important to punctuate the late shift with something enjoyable. Between six and midnight, one operator stayed in the office to catch any urgent messages, but after working at Whitehall for three years, Thaniel had never seen anything come through after eight. Once, there had been a strange, meaningless percussion from the Foreign Office, but that had been an accident: somebody had sat on the machine at the other end of the wire. Sat and bounced, he supposed, but people did all kind of odd things when nobody was watching. So, in the absence of any other landmark in the long six hours, he had made it a ritual to creep down to the canteen at nine o' clock and boil a kettle on one of the big ranges that were never quite cold.

It was November now. Thaniel curled his fingers round his cup to soak up the last of the heat. On the desk in front of him, his open watch ticked around to quarter past ten. The minute hand got stuck and wobbled urgently for a moment before falling down to half past. He set the cup aside and turned a page of yesterday's *Illustrated London News*. He only read the news while he was on the late shift, and he had hoped for some kind of spectacular military cock-up, but instead there was only the Duke of Edinburgh's visit to Croydon. Curling up in his chair, he hunched down into his coat and tried to think of warmer places than Croydon. His breath steamed.

He jumped when one of the telegraphs came to life. There were twelve in all, each connected to a different Whitehall department, and when he looked, he expected to see the movement from the machine wired to the Foreign Office. But it wasn't the Foreign Office; it was Great Scotland Yard. Thaniel leaned across to hold the edge of the transcript paper, which was in the habit of scrunching itself up after three inches, and felt uneasy.

Before the message started, there was a long, uncertain silence from the operator at the other end. Thaniel would have been willing to bet that he knew who it was. Superintendent Williamson coded in the same hesitant way in which he spoke. When the message finally did start, it was jerky and full of pauses.

Irish group Clan na Gael – has left me a note promising that – they will detonate bombs in all public buildings on – 30th May. Williamson.

Thaniel pulled the telegraph key towards him. He was a good telegraphist and he could type Morse code at forty-five words per minute, but it felt far too slow now. *Please confirm message.*

There was another pause. *Just found – note on my desk. Promises to blow me off my stool on 30th May. Signed Clan na Gael.*

Thaniel sat still for a moment. Adolphus Williamson was the head of Special Irish Branch, and therefore a natural target for angry Fenians. He sent all his own telegrams, and when he knew he was speaking to a familiar operator, he signed himself Dolly, as if they were all part of the same gentlemen's club. Thaniel couldn't help feeling protective over somebody called Dolly. *Are you all right?*

Yes. A long silence. *Must admit – a bit shaken. Going home.*

Be careful.

Thank you.

by Natasha Pulley

While the sounder was still clicking out the superintendent's last word, Thaniel picked up the transcript again and hurried through the dark corridor beyond the office to a door at the far end, under which firelight bled. He knocked, then opened it. Inside, the senior clerk looked up and scowled.

'I'm not here. This had better be important.'

'It's from the Yard, sir.'

The senior clerk snatched the transcript. Having begun service as his office, the room now looked slept-in with its collection of books and blankets heaped on the floor. He claimed that he stayed because his wife snored, but Thaniel was starting to think that she must have forgotten about him by now and changed the locks. Once he had read the note, he nodded.

'All right, Steepleton. You can go home. I'd better tell the Home Secretary.'

Thaniel left, quickly.

Home was a boarding house just north of Millbank Prison. It was a short walk from Whitehall. Under the gas lamps, a thin mist pawed at the windows of the closed shops, which became steadily shabbier nearer home. The air was biting, but he was glad to be outside. He couldn't help reflecting that the Home Office was probably the largest public building in London. Others had already had the same thought. Last March, some Irishmen had tried to throw a bomb in through a ground floor window. They'd missed and managed only to blow up some bicycles in the street outside, but in the telegraphy office, the bang had knocked Thaniel's teeth together. *All public buildings* sounded like the threat of a far more organised group than that.

As usual, a beggar was sleeping under the boarding house's wide porch. He grunted when Thaniel went by.

'Evening, George,' Thaniel whispered.

'Gngh,' said George.

He climbed the wooden stairs as quietly as he could. Inside, the boarding house was not as bleak as it looked; the damp and the fog had streaked the outer walls with mildew, but the rooms inside were plain and neat, each with a bed, a stove, and a plumbed sink. By rule of the landlady, the fifteen boarders were all single men, and given a bed and one meal a day for the flat annual cost of fifty pounds. Very much the same as the inmates of the prison next door. Thaniel felt angry about that sometimes, but less towards the government than towards himself. He had meant to do better in life than a prisoner.

At the top of the steps, his door was already ajar.

He stopped breathing. Everything seemed silent, but somebody else could have been holding his breath inside too. After standing for what felt like hours, Thaniel pushed the door open with his fingertips and stood sharply back. No one came out. Leaving the door open for the light, he snatched a match from the dresser and struck it against the wall, his fingertips unsteady from a mixture of fear and of sudden resentment towards the landlady, who refused to put in gas lights. While he held the match to the lamp wick, the back of his neck pricked and burned with the certainty that somebody was about to shove past him. The lamp caught with a sigh.

The room looked as it always did.

His back against the wall, Thaniel stood holding the burned-down match. The charred head crumbled off and hit the linoleum with a tap, leaving a smudge of black dust. He had to work up some nerve to look under the fold-down bed and in the narrow wardrobe, but they were empty too. Feeling calmer, he checked the savings he kept under the loose floorboard for his sister, who lived off an army pension. Undisturbed. It took him a little while to notice that the kettle was steaming. After crossing the room in five steps he put his fingertips against the side of it. It was hot, not warm, and when he opened the stove door, the coals glowed.

The crockery on the worktop was gone. He paused. It took a desperate burglar to steal unwashed dishes. Thaniel's relationship with washing-up was similar to his relationship with his sister: dutiful but unwilling, with direct contact reduced to a biannual basis. He opened the cupboard to see if they had taken the cutlery too, and blinked when he found the missing plates and bowls stacked inside.

by Natasha Pulley

They were still warm to touch. He left them and searched everything again. Nobody would break into a flat on the third floor merely in order to do his washing-up. But it seemed that they had. Perplexed, he went back downstairs. The cold outside felt sharper than it had a few minutes ago.

'George! George,' he said, giving the beggar a shake. The smell of sweat rose from his clothes. 'My flat's been burgled. Was it you?'

'You haven't got anything worth stealing,' George growled.

'Did you see anyone?'

'I might have done.'

'I …' Thaniel went through his pockets. 'I've got four pence and an elastic band.'

George sighed and sat up in his nest of blankets and newspapers. 'I didn't properly see, did I? I was asleep. Or I was trying.'

'So you saw …'

'Pair of boots,' he said, and took the coins.

'I see,' said Thaniel, doing his best not to sound annoyed. George looked like he had been middle-aged when time began, and however annoying he was, Thaniel's thoughts rebelled at the idea of snapping at an old man. 'But lots of people live here, how do you know it wasn't one of them?'

George shot him an irritable look. 'If you spent all day begging down here on the ground, you'd know everyone's boots. None of you have got brown ones.'

Thaniel had not met all of his neighbours, but he was inclined to believe George. As far as he understood, they were all clerks of some kind, all members of the crowd of grey coats and black hats that swamped London for half an hour every morning and evening around office work hours. Without meaning to, he looked down at his own black shoes, where a thick layer of polish hid the scuff marks.

'Anything else? Anything at all?' he said.

'Christ, what'd he take that was so important?'

'Nothing.'

George looked exasperated. 'What do you care, then? It's late, some of us want to get some sleep before the constable turfs us out at the crack of dawn.'

'Mystery man breaks into my flat, does the washing-up and takes nothing, I'd like to know why!'

'Sure it wasn't your mum?'

'She's dead.'

George sighed. 'Small brown boots. Maybe a boy.'

'I want my four pence back.'

'Bugger off,' George yawned, and lay back down again.

Thaniel went out onto the empty street with a half-formed hope of seeing a boy in brown boots vanishing around the corner, but there was nobody. Unwillingly, he turned back inside. Taken twice in a row, the three flights of steps made his thighs ache.

Back in his room, he flicked open the door of the stove again to let the heat out and sat down on the edge of the bed, his hands held out towards the coals. It was only then that he saw the velvet box on his pillow. It had been tied with a white ribbon, from which hung a label that said 'To Mr Steepleton'. He pulled off the ribbon and tilted the box open. Inside was a pocket watch.

He lifted it out. It wouldn't open when he pressed the catch. Puzzled, he held it to his ear, but the clockwork was dead and the spindle wouldn't wind. His fingertips caught over an engraving on the back.

For the 30th of May, 1884.

....

Natasha Pulley is from Cambridgeshire. She studied English at Oxford and turned down an offer from Beijing University in order to come to UEA. She has published a few historical short stories in online collections, and is now working on a novel about a pianist and a prescient watchmaker.

by Natasha Pulley

Eliza Robertson

Feathertramp (working title)
An excerpt

My novel is about 19-year-old Marisol, who leaves Dawson City, Yukon after assisting her grandfather's suicide. Her rides have led her to Alaska, but she has decided to head south to find her best friend in Vancouver. The excerpt begins on her final day in Anchorage, where she has been making cash as a 'gum and graffiti buster.'

Her hostel did not offer breakfast, but it was Saturday, which meant the Baptists parked their station wagons outside with toasters and Wonderbread and vats of sour, filtered coffee. Their napkins had bible verses. *The Lord is my strength and song, and he is become my salvation.* Exodus 15:2. *If God is for us, who is against us?*

Marisol chose a blueberry bagel. The girl beside her ate toast. When the girl reached for the marmalade, her elbow knocked Marisol's apple juice. They each grabbed a stack of napkins. *Be still and know that I am God*, the ink bleeding into juice. *To fear the Lord is the begging of freedom.*

After her bagel, she examined a map. She couldn't see the highway to Juneau, so she unfolded the insert of south east Alaska. That didn't help either. When a woman with a dishrag over her shoulder asked if she'd like tea, Marisol presented it to her.

'Which is the highway to Juneau?' she asked.

The woman set down the teapot and wiped her hands on her apron. 'There is none, hun.'

'Hm?'

'There's no land access. You can fly in or take the ferry.'

'Hm?'

'The ferry's nice. Real scenic.'

'Expensive,' said the Australian boy on the other side of Marisol. Australian or New Zealander – she could never tell.

'Get what you pay for,' said the woman. She lifted her pot and offered him tea.

'Well how do you get to British Columbia, then?' said Marisol.

'Glenn Highway. North,' said the Australian.

'But I just came from north,' said Marisol. 'I want to go south.'

'Have to go north to go south,' said the woman with the tea.

So Marisol left the hostel with her pack and a styrofoam cup of thin coffee. She walked east on 26th Street until she found the visitor information bureau. The woman there said the same as the Australian. North on the Glenn Highway to Tok Junction, and then the Alaska Highway across the border. Marisol didn't bother to reply. She dropped into one of the olive polyester chairs by the brochure racks and stared at the map of the world tacked to the wall. Visitors had pushed pins into their home cities. Red-beaded pins, into the United States, into Canada, too many pins for the island of Japan. Some of the pins had dropped out, or someone had removed them – the surface of Europe like braille. She stared at this map, and the pins, and the fat black fly that bumped against the window, and she thought she could pin the fly to the map. She could pin the fly to the red dot of Anchorage. One of the information counsellors had taped a red arrow there. *You are here!* with an exclamation point. *You are here! You are here!*

So with five days behind her, she hitch-hiked the way she came. She paid one dollar and seventy-five cents for the bus to Centennial Park, and then she waited on the highway road shoulder. She didn't lower her pack. She didn't hold the sign. She didn't stick out her thumb. Her hip, maybe. Maybe she stuck out her hip. She wore her loose pale jeans, which had loosened more since she left, and a breezy cotton crop-top. She waited with her arms folded and watched the cars. She searched the windows for the drivers' eyes, and sometimes they glanced at her, and sometimes they didn't notice, but all the cars passed, except a silver Ford Focus, which slowed for her to cross.

by Eliza Robertson

She did cross, out of embarrassment, and then she waited for a gap in the Anchorage-bound traffic to jaywalk back across the road. She thumbed after that. She trailed backward along the highway, watched the cars, the sun off their windshields. She gave them twenty minutes. Twenty minutes for one of the windshields to stop. She timed the cars by her yellow cereal box wristwatch. A woman pulled over after fourteen. She drove a mini van with two pink-snouted boxers in the back. She was headed all the way to Glennallen, so Marisol climbed in.

The woman worked as a substitute teacher, she said, but jobs were scarce, so she travelled. She had just spent a week in Anchorage at Pacific Northern Academy. The school offers fencing, she said. 'The eight year olds. The eight year olds are fencing.'

They listened to an author read a story on National Public Radio until they lost the signal. One of the dogs tried to scramble over the console into Marisol's lap. He smelled sour. A pearl of saliva swung off his lip. Marisol ignored him. She watched the blue road that ran like film tape, like an audience pressed rewind. Five-day backtrack, beneath the mountains and low floss of cloud. The dwarfed pines, too soft-needled to look woodsy. You could spend your life this way – on wrong turns and false starts, from car to car, for years and kilometres. It would be easy to stay lost.

From Eureka Summit, you could see four ranges. Mountains named in Inuit and Athabascan languages, Chugach, Talkeetna, which meant *where the rivers join*. She could not see the peaks – too much mist. But it would be a nice view for planes. She'd always liked how they made elbow-shaped islands on the other side of the sky.

On descent from the summit, the woman stopped the van in the centre of the road. She pressed her palm over the slats of her bob while she stared out the windshield to the far side of the highway. Marisol could only see the slope, the stiff thickets of copper roadbush. But then the bush juddered, and a white spectre of a sheep froze behind the brambles.

'Dall sheep,' said the woman. She glanced at the rear-view mirror, then returned her eyes to the road.

Marisol stared at the ram as they rolled past. Those great coiling horns, how the bone actually corkscrews. Sunlight reeling off the ram's coat.

*

When you walk through Glennallen, all you see is Mount Drum. Stratovolcano at the end of the line, conical and breath-stealing. You can't help but look up. She remembers this impulse from Anglican cathedrals. In London, with her Granddad, when she was five or six. Tourists ambled in, and their chins all lifted. Eyes running over sunlit saints, the rib-vaulted ceilings. Here, it's lava and snow domes. Twelve thousand feet of ice and old rock.

At Sparks General Store in Glennallen, she bought beef jerky, two litres of water and a freakshow apple the size of two fists. She chewed the jerky outside on the curb. A neon sign said, *Auto Repair Shop and Cellphone Store. X-Men First Class on DVD. Also have Thor!* Another sign advertised game bags. Ten dollars for Moose or a four-pack for thirty. Caribou bags, twenty-five. The biggest sign was for ammunition, written in capital letters. *SOFT-CORE REMINGTON AMMO. GREAT PRICES ON AMMO. SHOTGUN AMMO FOR BIRDS AND SLUGS.*

She waited on the side of the road for two hours. You can panic in two hours, on the gravel between trees and the highway, the bears and the mountains. She'd seen bears – Dawson City dumpster divers, a black bear outside Tasty's once, his head plugged inside a jar of jumbo pickles. But she'd never seen a wolf. Forty-five hundred wolves in the Yukon and she'd never seen one. You never knew how close you were, in the brush between pines, when you can't see the sky or ahead of you ten feet. And here on the road shoulder, four cars in two hours – you wondered where you'd camp. And is it still camping if you don't have a tent? At what point do you lie in the dirt and call it *Shit I'm stranded in the woods.*

She played jacks with gravel. Dropped the ball from her pocket

by Eliza Robertson

and snatched rocks, assigned arbitrary points per stone in her palm. Each time a car rounded the corner, she scrambled to her feet, punched out her thumb and watched them pass. The man who stopped drove a sun-cracked blue cargo van. He didn't unroll the window or open the passenger door, so she hovered at the side of the van and tried to peer in. A straw hat domed over the headrest, and she could see the arc of his shoulders in papery denim. There were no seats in the rear of his van, but a metal floor. Then she saw his eyes on her in the rear-view, so she heaved open the sliding door and climbed in. The floor was scattered with bulrushes – fifteen or twenty clipped fresh from the pond. She stepped between the stalks and ducked for a closer look – the seedy spikes on their shafts like candlesticks.

'Hi,' she said, as she climbed over the console and plunked into the front seat. 'Thank you for stopping.'

He nodded once, but didn't otherwise respond. He wore jeans the same pale blue as his shirt, and the denim sunk in hollow lulls off his thigh and the caps of his knees. She couldn't pinpoint his age. Sixties, maybe. The corners of his mouth stained a rheumy yellow, crusted with the same oily nuggets you collect in the corner of your eye.

She lowered her eyes to her lap, then out the window. She could hear the bulrushes hush against the metal floor. 'Do you collect them?' she asked. 'The bulrushes.'

He kept his stare on the road and reached his hand for the rear-view mirror. A tube dangled there – she hadn't noticed. He drew the tube toward him and plugged the grey clips into his nose. He breathed in. She couldn't see the respirator, but it gurgled with his exhale. She looked away.

'My mother makes bouquets,' he said.

She nodded at the window and tried to spot the reflection of his breathing apparatus. She could only see the tube. How he kept the cannula looped off the rear-view mirror like an air-freshener.

They didn't speak for ten minutes. Then, he told her he was fifty-five. He said he had smoked crack for thirty years and weed for forty, but he was clean now, too late. He said he was American, but lived in Canada half his life. When he was seventeen he bought a 1960

Feathertramp

Chevy pickup, and drove to Long Beach on Vancouver Island, the Pacific Rim. You could camp on the beach, then, he said. You could drink cheap sherry and Labatt Blue till the tide went out, and then you could climb into your pickup and drive donuts in the sand.

Eliza Robertson was born in Vancouver, Canada, and completed her undergraduate degree at the University of Victoria. Her stories have appeared in journals in Canada, the UK and the United States, and have been shortlisted for National Magazine Awards and the McClelland & Stewart Journey Prize. She is working on her first novel and gathering stories for a collection.

by Eliza Robertson

Sara Sha'ath

Shrieking Gulls
An extract from a novel in progress, set in 1920s Southampton. In this chapter, Martha, a recently widowed mother of four, sets out with her daughter Jane to sell baked goods to the migrant workers reclaiming land for the New Docks.

The duck boards over the mud flats were precarious, just a collection of haphazardly placed planks stretching all the way from the rail track to the pumping station. Martha and Jane were walking on borrowed land; the spoils of years of battle between man and sea. As they stepped on each duck, light brown sludge bubbled and seeped through the gaps and holes.

In the distance, Martha could see a row of fifteen or twenty heads, little more than dots, and pink tones suggesting shirts off in the sunshine. The workers had stopped for lunch. Behind them the dark bulk of pumping equipment was still, hydraulic elbows paused mid-punch.

'It's like shells,' Jane said, looking at the shimmering fan shapes in the mud, left by the spitting chute of the dredger. It might have been beautiful if it weren't for the stench of refuse. At the other end of the site, they were filling the land with the contents of Southampton's dust carts and drains, crushing the waste with mechanical rollers before dumping the soft dredged silt over the top. The smell was burnt-out, rancid.

Overhead, seagulls shrieked. Martha kept her eyes low, holding her baking tray as level as she could. The pasties they had made that morning were still steaming, tucked under her whitest tea towel to keep off the flies.

'Be careful,' Martha said as Jane took a sliding step.

'I'm being careful, Mum. It's slimy.'

'Just be careful.'

Martha had one eye on her feet and one on the row of mud-spattered, scrawny-legged workers ahead of them. She'd heard that some of them had travelled from as far away as Wales, work was so scarce. They lived in a shanty town of disused crates and lean-to shelters at one end of the site. She felt for them; even now, at the height of summer, a night by the water would be cold and exposed. Martha heard a shout, so faint on the breeze she wasn't sure if it was a gull; she looked up. The men looked like they were staring back at her, but the sun was too bright for her to tell.

When they reached the platform, they were met by a man in an oil-stained vest with salt and pepper hair. His sunburned shoulders were peeling, greyish flakes curling away from boiled-pink flesh beneath.

'You want to watch yourselves on them ducks,' he said, helping Martha up the steps. 'Plenty of men stronger than you two been swallowed up by that mud.'

He took Jane by her elbow, courteous, but a little too close for Martha's liking.

'Fall off it at night. One too many, most likely. Nothing left by morning but a cap floating on the mud and a pay packet sitting lonely in the foreman's office.'

'Don't they call out for help?' Jane asked.

'That's enough of that,' Martha said, guiding Jane away. 'She doesn't need scaring.'

Now she was close, she could see she'd timed it perfectly; as well as the row of workers at the edge of the platform there was another ten or so just knocking off, finding a spot in the sun to stuff their pipes or unpack sorry-looking bits of lunch from pound tobacco tins. Martha smiled. The relief of being on solid ground made it easy to smile.

'Pasties,' she said, trying for the singsong tone of the Tuesday market men. 'Best pork pasties. Still warm. Tuppence each.'

The man in the vest tugged at the edge of Martha's tea towel.

'No you don't,' she said. 'That'll be tuppence first, thank you very much.'

by Sara Sha'ath

He grinned and put grubby fingers into his pocket for the change.

'She sounds like my mum,' he said over his shoulder, raising a murmur of laughter.

'She sounds like my missus,' said the man next to him, drawing close to put two pocket-warm pennies in Martha's hand.

'She don't look like your missus.'

'Don't I know it. More's the shame.'

Someone said something Martha didn't quite hear. They all laughed, loud this time. She felt her cheeks flush redder, but she pretended not to notice, taking the cloth off her tray. The smell of freshly-baked pastry rose into the warm air.

After they'd sold more than half the pasties to men who queued with surprising patience and good grace, they walked a circuit of the platform, Martha taking the money and Jane holding the tray. She stood close, not venturing far beyond the circumference of her mother's hem. Martha tried to ignore resentful looks from workers who didn't have tuppence to spare. Some glowered, most avoided eye contact altogether. At the periphery of her vision she noticed small details: bits of mud-caked sacking tied to feet; a bruise, the size of an iron, splashed across a shoulder blade; a tattooed woman legs splayed, eels for hair; a head resting listless against the wall, neck too tired to support it. They stepped over a man lying still in the sun, ribcage like a half-built ship. He could have been sunbathing or dead. She pulled Jane a little closer, tried to keep the confidence in her voice.

'Pork pasties. Tuppence each.' She had misjudged it. They would never sell another dozen. Martha felt a trickle of panic in her chest. In the kitchen, when it was just her and the stove and a bright idea, she'd been confident she could make this work. She would make some money – enough for a week's groceries – and get her first good night's sleep in weeks.

As they rounded the corner of the station, they stepped into the shadow of the pumps and felt the cool relief of shade, though here the smell of refuse was worse. There were stooped figures clambering over piles of rubbish, heads bent down, looking for anything salvageable – old clothes, scrap metal. About fifty yards away, there

Shrieking Gulls

was a man with a rusty pram, picking among the ash from the clinker trucks. He was almost completely black from head to toe. He looked their way, his eyes bright white against his filthy skin.

'Looking for coal. Bits that ain't been burned.'

She turned away from the scavenger to see a young man next to her who had spoken. He was one of four standing in the shade with neither tobacco nor lunch. They weren't much older than Luke. The one who had just spoken moved gingerly, a skinny lad with joints too big for his limbs. His trousers were torn, revealing running sores on his legs. The gaps between his fingers were in much the same state. Martha wondered if it was just impetigo or something infectious. If it had been Luke, she would have had him at home resting with a cold press on those sores. She felt a pang of distress for him and yet his expression made her draw closer to Jane. All four of the boys had their hungry eyes on the pasties left on the tray. Martha could see they needed them, probably hadn't eaten in days, but the painstaking sums in her housebook said it wasn't her concern.

'The pasties are tuppence, boys. I can only sell them for tuppence.'

'One penny. I'll give you a penny for two,' he said.

Martha wasn't going to be drawn in. She knew they didn't have a farthing between them. She tried to arrange the cloth back over the top of the tray and ushered Jane round the corner. They followed.

'Give us one.'

'I'm starving.'

'I'll have it tomorrow. I'll give you sixpence tomorrow. A shilling.'

Martha felt a hand on her elbow and instinctively pulled away. She almost tripped on the tallest of the lads who'd circled round to the other side of them.

'Mum!' One of the lads was taking the tray from Jane's hands. She jerked it out of his reach and walked faster.

'You stay away,' Martha said, trying to keep the anxiety from her voice. She spread her arms wide in front of Jane.

'You stay away,' the boy with the sores mimicked and his hand shot past her.

She saw him taking a bite, his cracked lips closing round pastry,

by Sara Sha'ath

and her arms moved before she knew what she was doing. She pushed him hard, so hard he hit the floor face first with a dull crunch. The pasty broke into pieces on the mud-flaked boards. Martha's breath stopped solid in her throat.

'Oi, enough of that. Leave them alone.'

Two or three of the older workers walked over and all of the lads, apart from the one on the floor backed off. Martha watched, horrified, as he got to his knees and started picking up the mush of pastry, scooping it into his mouth as fast as he could. His cheek was bruised, blood spotting, spots joining into drips. She had done that.

'Don't worry about them, love. Little pricks don't know how to treat a lady.'

Martha half-turned, barely registering the man in the vest. She couldn't take her eyes off the boy, licking bits of mud and onion off one hand while the other now clutched his face. The man in the vest picked up her tea towel from the floor, folded it neatly with his tattooed fingers and handed it back. Then he touched her face, just gently, stroking two rough fingers under her chin. It was a long time since Martha had been touched like that. It felt as though his fingers had left a mark, a tingling trail of sweat or grease. He smiled, showing blood red gums, yellow teeth.

'What's for lunch tomorrow?' he asked.

Martha took a breath and thought about the coins in her purse. She became aware that Jane was clutching her arm. She took the tray and held her hand, though she wasn't sure for whose benefit.

'Kidney pies tomorrow,' she said.

With shaking hands and a thumping heart, Martha managed to sell a few more pasties then got the two of them off the platform as soon as she could. Her purse was heavy in her pocket. She'd thought she'd feel good about it – she wanted to show the boys they wouldn't have to worry – but instead she felt a little sick.

'I'm sorry, Jane,' she said. 'I won't make you do that again, I promise.'

Jane was staring at the mud, her face bleached. Martha thought about the boy's bruised cheek, blood spots ballooning. They walked the boards in silence.

When they were almost back to the tracks, Jane put an arm out to stop her and pointed at the ground. Crossing the boards by their feet was a tiny army of sludge-coated pea crabs, glistening in the sun. They zigzagged their way back to the ocean, regrouping, following the rivulets of seawater sweating from the flats.

'The ocean will take what it's owed,' Martha said, under her breath.

A loud, shuddering growl made them both start. The pumps were back in action, pounding the water from the earth. Soon the pile drivers would join in too – a clamour of industry to drown out the crash of the waves.

....

Sara Sha'ath grew up in the South East and read English Literature at Cardiff University. In 2011, she received the David Higham Award. She lives in London and is currently working on a novel.

by Sara Sha'ath

Kim Sherwood

A True Relation
Opening of a novel

1712

The South Hams spread around her like a sailor's sea-worn coat, spring fields threaded with sun-red earth and patched over by corn. This was her corner of England; all she'd ever known of the land. Church spires competed with trees to claim the skyline, and cattle lay in the fields, waiting for the distant cloud-bank to build and burst. Molly walked to the cliff edge, shielding her eyes against the ocean's glitter.

Thatched roofs clung to the coves, where crab men and fishing vessels drifted out for the day's catch. The water was flat, and the wind so gentle the boats did not have to tack in at all. It was the kind of day to lean on the poop deck railing and let the sea-salt breeze tighten her smile until it was numb. She looked from Thurlestone Rock, giant and isolated in the low tide, to Burgh Island, where The Pilchard Inn milled with men waiting for the next shoal. Beyond, a Customs cutter inched towards Dartmouth, overshadowing passing yawls. If it was patrolling for smugglers bold enough to land in the daytime, Molly thought, it would need God's own luck to catch them going at that speed. Especially if it were Tom West they were hoping to stop.

Since returning to land, she'd tried to ignore the sounds of the sea: its waves no longer lullaby, hymn, nor love song, and the stories that passed from ship to ship along its ancient paths no longer hers to collect. She needed now to hear instead the tales buried in these green lanes: the tracks of animal and man, the coded birdsong, the wildflower hedgerows that spoke of sun and rainfall. Not just hear them, but love them, no matter how much these mud-soaked skirts weighed her down. Gathering up her dress and shift, Molly pulled back from the horizon and set off towards Bantham.

The village was busy this morning, its one street full of noise and steam as women bent over their laundry in open doorways or carried fish to the salting house. Joining the village from the cliff path, Molly saw a boy and girl with a basket of eggs try to trip each other up. They were perhaps ten years younger than her, aged six or seven. She wondered which woman eyeing her now was their mother, and what concoction of thatch and pottage would always stand for them as home. Mud sucked at her legs, and she wanted to let it hold her back from the beach ahead, to keep her from discovering what smells or sounds might have burrowed into her as a child. But she walked on to the sand dunes, where a path dropped through the brush grasses to Bantham Beach.

The River Avon began and ended here, both estuary mouth and inlet snaking into the hills. Molly squelched across the sand, following the crescents drawn by the ocean's retreat to the exposed estuary bed. The rotten stench of sun-baked seaweed took her back to Roscof. Picking her way to the bank, she trailed her hand over the slick rocks that buttressed the hillside, testing their solidity. Her grip tightened on the lichens when she saw what she'd been looking for.

A single cottage was tucked into the hillside facing the estuary. The location was just as Molly imagined, but the cottage looked nothing like the descriptions she'd read in Grace's diary. The chimney slumped into the collapsed sink of the roof, which was missing great tufts of thatch. The front had a mottled appearance, the red rubble-stone and cocoa-coloured cob blemishes against the surviving lime wash. Taking a deep breath – the kind she once would have drawn before diving into unknown depths – Molly went closer. Battered dry-stone-walling marked where the vegetable patch had been lost to the high tide. She climbed over it, cursing the brush of stinging nettles. The curly kale and runner beans she had imagined watching grow with Grace were nowhere to be seen. Instead, shells and seaweed crunched under her feet. Nothing she'd read about had lasted.

The front door was warped. Molly forced it open, meeting a wall

by Kim Sherwood

of dust. Pulling her cap off, she held it over her mouth – tasting her fear on the damp rim – and let the dust envelop her. The floorboards in the cross-passage groaned beneath her. There was a door on the left and she ducked under the beam into the hot stink of moth-eaten pelts and crusted bird droppings. Sunbeams fell through the rafters, spotlighting the rotten lesions mapped across the walls. In the corner, a clump of fallen thatch had been used by a birthing doe. Molly could see the delicate skull of a failed faun peeping from the hay; one empty eye-socket still fringed with fur, warning her away. She ignored it, looking from the bare hearth to a broken bookshelf that lay nearby like a pile of kindling. Other oak remnants – a table, a dresser – were bound with weeds, which climbed through the floorboards. Molly picked up a remaining slat of the bookshelf, finding carved flowers and hearts. Was this her father's work, or did Tom carefully apply his knife to these signs of love?

Molly turned in the centre of the wreckage. No memories threatened or welcomed her. There was nothing. She turned to search the other rooms when changing clouds overhead redrew the sunbeams, and something silver winked between the floorboards. Molly knelt down. The wood had worn away, leaving gaps. Wedging her fingers between the boards, she tried to pull them up, but they would not give. There was a poker amongst the weeds, and she wedged it into the fissure. The wood splintered with such suddenness she fell backwards. She'd achieved a slot big enough for her knuckles, and then her wrist, with her arm paling for lack of blood. Molly groped blindly beneath the floor, trying to identify what she was touching: cobwebs, roots, frightened insects. And then something solid. She pulled the object free.

It was a gilt-silver fork engraved with curled ivy. Molly ran her thumb over its grooves. She had felt the exact same twist of soft metal on the spoon she'd used at ship meals every day for as long as she remembered.

Diary Entry

I left home today. I shall never be allowed back. I shall never be received in society. I have defied the laws of King and God. I am eighteen years of age.

I commit these thoughts to paper because words seem to determine everything. My father told me that for a woman to write her own story, her own poetry, was unnatural. He told me that any story of my life is but ink poured into a great pit, lacking such worthy deeds as enlighten the pens of great men.

I left because I could not live with that as truth. I left because staying would have meant a life of locked doors and locked lips; a life of pain, whether pain held inside, or pain felt on the flesh; a life that was not willingly mine.

I rely on Christopher now. Can we create the home we whispered of in those breathless moments hidden by the harpsichord's song, or the controlled wilderness of the garden?

We have come to Bantham. The coast is strange to me, and the people who live along it even stranger, though my home on the moors is only thirty miles away. I feel like Drake, standing on the beach of a new world. What life we could have here, if our fancies were made real. Christopher talks of building a grand establishment once he has received his estates. What life shall we have? What manner of husband will Christopher be? And what wife I? Now I look upon it I am visited by how truly little we know of men before we marry, and how little I know of myself.

Myself. I am a post-script, a name without meaning on my father's family tree. The legal deeds that sign my body over to my father's treasury; the marriage licence Christopher procured; even the tales told about me in the village fold me, invisible, into the history of others. Shall I not have my own story?

A True Relation of My Life and Deeds, Grace Tucker, June 3rd 1690

by Kim Sherwood

1699 – 1703

I.

New Year's Eve, 1699

A storm had rolled in from the channel to soak the last seconds of the century. Wind and rain joined the high tide, waves blanketing Bantham Beach to slam against the hillsides. The River Avon surged, breaking its banks, into the South Hams. The water destroyed Grace Tucker's garden, ripping up the cradled buds and nurtured roots, finally to push the front door open, letting the violence in.

Grace stood before the struggling fire. It was the centre of her house, black from providing heat for food and light for the table, which was stained too, with ink spills and the scratches of a child's first pen strokes. Now the flames were reduced to embers by the storm, just as the kitchen seemed to shrink with both men stood at either end, boxing her in.

Benedict hovered in the doorway, soaked through, and Grace thought she glimpsed dried blood on his hands. On the far side of the room, Tom leant against Molly's bedroom door. The column of his body collapsed inwards, those huge shoulders dragging on a failing back. In one hand, he held her diary. In the other, a pistol. Grace tried to keep her hands pinned to her skirts, but kept returning to pick at a loose thread.

'Please, Tom,' she said. 'I do not understand what has happened.'

Tom raised the book. In the firelight, he could just make out where Grace had pressed ink into its hide, embedding her words: *A True Relation of My Life and Deeds*.

'I remember one night, you saying you wanted to write for your bread,' he said. 'I laughed. I never thought you meant it. You must have kept this little confessional somewhere safe when I came around. Strange, to find it out tonight, with all the fineries I bought you. As if you was packing. And with my name on nearly every page. So now I know what a woman has to write about. Gossip, and the secrets of men.'

'It has only my life,' said Grace. 'I have written it for Molly. And – and for myself. There is nothing strange in that, nor harmful. Now please, tell me why you have come here so late.'

In the doorway, Benedict eased from foot to foot. He had never met Tom's lover before. None of the crew had. Whenever they came ashore, the ship burdened with barrels of brandy or chests of tea, Tom came here. The crew all talked about it: Tom West and his lover, a woman with a child begot by another man. But never in front of Tom. No one told him he was a lucky devil, a lady of quality to lie with whenever he wished, or said how strange it was, Tom caring for a girl with nothing of his blood in her veins. This was more than a warm bed and pottage in the morning, though. Benedict understood that now, but not why Tom had come here. What could this cottage mean to the men they'd dragged from the river, smugglers and Revenue bleeding alike? He shuffled back.

'I can wait outside,' he said. 'The horses –'

Tom cut through him, rolling Grace's gentle vowels in his Devon growl: 'No harm in it, you say. Then I take it there are none of my movements scribbled down in this masterpiece of yours?'

'What do you mean?' said Grace.

'A little late to play the fool, my girl.'

'I am playing at nothing.'

'No?' said Tom. 'Then it weren't your wretched words that got me and my men ambushed tonight?'

....

Kim Sherwood is working on a first novel. She hopes to become a literary author incorporating multiple genres. Kim studied Literature with Creative Writing at UEA, receiving the Jarrold Prize for outstanding performance, and continued onto the MA. Kim has been awarded a Studentship for UEA's Creative Writing PhD.

by Kim Sherwood

Dennison Smith

Seeds
An excerpt from a novel in progress

Her teenage son shouted from the driveway, 'Troglodyte! Get the fuck out here!'

Connie bellowed out the dormer, 'You don't know the meaning of that word!' She knew what she was – an old drunk, hiding away from the rising heat – but she wouldn't have him saying so.

The window rattled in its casement, its dehydrated putty dropping to the sill in nuggets. Having replaced three packs of Marlboro Menthols with one pack of nicotine gum, she stuck chunks on the window ledge to re-chew later. Since breaking a tooth, she'd never mistake a hunk of putty for gum again. Her mouth, like her window, was sucked dry by the awful change in the weather. At fifty-one, she was pickled: the outcome of gin and spleen.

She stared out the cyclopic dormer. The dusty arroyo snaked to the west like a grave dug for a giant rattler. She shook her head at her ugly metaphors, her mind corroded by late night TV while books lined her walls as makeshift insulation against the increasing heat. She saw beside the empty riverbed a line of cottonwoods – dead – and the garden that grew sage brush and smokethorn.

The brush fires had bypassed her hundred acres, but the real estate agents hadn't. They salivated around her boundary markers like dogs round the dumpsters behind the Higgly Piggly. She liked to say that – Higgly Piggly – but she didn't like to go there. From her home, she could just see the valley subdivisions where water, pumped from the sputtering Colorado River, continued to fill Jacuzzis though nothing grew anymore. Not even winter rye. Not even blue corn. She used to keep pigs and sheep and laying chicken, but in the end slaughtered every one of them. The farm was hardly a farm anymore. Her children were hardly children.

'Fucking fuck, are you coming?!' Her son's deep voice shot through the dormer window.

Connie shot back, 'Keep your pants on, boy! I'm coming!' and disappeared into the darkness where she screwed up her hair with bobby pins and plopped an over-sized sun hat on her head.

'Fuck Connie! Fuck! Motherfuck!'

Her son hadn't called her mother. Both her children had called her by her first name since the day they could speak, as if she had no greater distinction than being the tallest amongst them. But while they grew fast as suckers on a willow tree, Connie got shorter every year. She was squat, square, with a shoddy thyroid. Shrivelled up by the blasted god of California: sunshine.

Tom was pounding the hood of the car. *Her* car. With his backpack on, he cast the same hunchback shadow that his father had. His utopian father had filled her with seed, then hightailed it out of town, so that by the time Connie gave birth, utopia and the father were gone.

'Hold your horses!' she screamed into the yard.

The bobby pins jabbed at her scalp. She leaned against the wall, wondering why on earth she was going to all this trouble for the no good boy. The boy was no good, and the walls could testify. His fist had slugged holes in the horsehair plaster that read like coupon punch cards in the wall. She should stay in her house, in her four safe walls; she should turn him over to the cops, sit back in her armchair and turn up the TV and wait for the kid in a Slurpy-stained smock to deliver her groceries to the door. But Tom was *her* boy. (The first birth was a boy. Two years later, a girl, by some other father, under the same California sky.)

'Tom's going to kill you if you don't get down there,' her daughter said, suddenly appearing in the door frame, a rifle in one hand and a ceramic piggy-bank in the other.

'Girl, goddamn, you scared me!'

Her daughter wore a stained frock with big pockets. Big boned,

by Dennison Smith

long-armed and long-legged, her sleeves too short for her strong wrists, and the hem of her dress riding above her dirty knees. Over her large breasts, the dress dropped straight down like a waterfall, though no one had seen a waterfall in years. And the man who spawned *that* child? A man with a handlebar moustache and soiled boxers who'd snuck down the stairs one morning and left through the screen door – a wet spot of oil on the gravel where his Oldsmobile stood all night, and a puddle on the Encyclopaedia Britannica where Tom took out his small boy's penis and peed on Connie's books.

Tom was always protective of Tam, even before she was born. Though Connie looked sourly at the two of them – Tam in the doorway with a rifle, Tom pounding on the car in the driveway – brother and sister were fiercely loyal, at least to each other. Loyal for shameful reasons, but loyal all the same. She had to give them that.

Having put on the sun hat, she yanked it off, grabbed the piggy bank from her daughter's hand and dropped it into the hat. 'Hit it with the butt of the rifle,' she ordered, and her daughter did as she was told. Now the faces of Lincoln and Washington and Jefferson and the shards of a broken pig filled the sun hat.

'Lend me another hat,' Connie said.

'What hat?' asked Tammy.

'Any damn hat. That sun out there's going to kill me.'

'I don't got one,' said Tammy, who was forever out in the hard pan of lizards and stalky weeds she called a garden without a hat. She would have looked sun-bronzed if it weren't for the dust, and though the sun had bleached her blonde hair white, unwashed, it darkened up again.

'Well get me a bottle of gin, girl!'

Tammy obeyed, but Connie knew better than to think she was a good girl.

'Fuck, it's about fucking time,' Tom said as Connie came out on the porch.

A fresh piece of gum in her mouth, shielding her eyes with her puffy hand, she blinked back at the one-eyed house whose sanctuary she was leaving for the first time in years. 'Tom-fool robs the Higgly Piggly on foot in the light of day! I'll be damned if I'm playing chauffeur now!' She chucked her son the car keys. They landed like buckshot in the dirt. 'Nothing even to show for your effort!' She had superior diction, and she used it to triumph over her foul-mouthed son. 'Dropped your loot in the parking lot and ran!' She stuck out her nicotine gum between her smoker's yellow teeth.

'Stay in your hole if you want to, Con,' said Tom, 'I'll drive my goddamn self, and I'll keep your fucking car! Don't expect me home till Hell freezes over!'

Water hadn't frozen in winter for years.

She never drove the damn thing anyway, but it was *her* car. *Her* son. Connie plunked her hat of coins on the rear by Tommy's duffel.

'What's that?!' he asked.

'Getaway money, what do you think, boy?!'

She climbed into the driver's seat and sniffed at the black ashtray that hung from its hinges and stank. She plucked the gum from her mouth and stuck it against the tray.

'I'm taking you as far as the Rio Grande. Then you're on your own.'

Tom grunted.

'Where's my gin?' she cried out the window at Tammy fighting with the front door. Tammy held up a gallon bottle. Despite her big tallness, she had the look of a little girl who had never quite got born. Born misplaced, Connie thought, born backwards actually. Connie remembered the pain of it with a shudder.

'The door won't lock,' said Tammy.

'Why are you locking the door?!' Connie shouted. 'You aren't coming with us! Tom,' she turned on her son, 'Your sister has no reason to come! She's not her brother's keeper!'

Tammy climbed into the back, beside the sun hat of petty cash. She put the rifle next to the gearshift and the bottle on her mother's lap.

Tom said, 'I want her.'

by Dennison Smith

A native man on the car radio recounted his tribe's origin story.

'There were many worlds. Our people came up through the worlds. The first world was red. Red ants lived here. Black beetles lived here. The world was small and dry and bad and spinning fast. People who lived here were dizzy. So our people climbed up through the hole in the sky.

The second world was blue. Blue birds and blue-tinted swallows lived here. It was a bad small dry world. The world spun fast and made the people dizzy, like drunks. There were no plants, no rivers or mountains. So our people climbed up through the hole in the sky.

The third world was a yellow world. Yellow grasshopper people lived here. The land was bare and made of cliffs. The rivers were dry and thin as spider's fingers. The spinning made the people dizzy and angry. They fought with each other because the world was small and dry and bad. Then they crawled up through the hole in the sky.

The fourth world was every colour. Red, blue, yellow, and black and white, but no sun or moon or stars. First Man and First Woman were born here. Here there was water, but too much water. Floods came, and our people crawled up through the hole in the sky.

This is the fifth world. The last. Here there is light and darkness. The Hero Twins were born here. Children of the sun, they travelled to the sun's house. They rid the world of monsters. You can still see dead monsters lying on the ground. Maybe you think that they are mountains. You can climb the mountains and feel very near the sky. But there are no more worlds. We are ordinary people and cannot get to the sky.'

On the transcontinental highway heading south, the car shook as the speedometer hit sixty. Connie grabbed for the gearshift to move into fourth but caught hold of the rifle instead. The coins jangled and the chassis rattled like an earthquake had begun, which would be a fit ending for Tom. Connie remembered too well how she'd shoved him out of her with the china breaking all around her twenty years ago. Now she edged the car up to sixty-one, afraid the sides of the vehicle would suddenly drop away. Though the blinker light was missing on the left, she couldn't accelerate high enough anyway to pass another car. She could have passed a tractor if there were any farmers.

'Never thought you'd leave, Tom,' Connie said, 'thought you were like the rats under the floorboards: here to stay. You know what you sound like with your fuck fuck fucks?'

'An outlaw,' said Tammy from the backseat.

'Don't I know that!' cried Connie, 'One child an outlaw, one an outcast! Your youth has gone to waste, and mine gone in your making!'

As a patrol car slowed beside them, Tom slumped into his seat and buried his face behind his muscular arm ringed with black tattoos. Connie shunted the liquor bottle underneath her legs, turned off the highway and veered down the lonely eastern side of a salt lake that had seeped away from its edges to reveal aluminum cans and tires. Under it lay Indian land and a flooded frontier town (flooded in the days of the dams and hydroelectric dreams) and the dormant monster, the San Andreas fault. On its far edges could be seen the water mains that, though they no longer irrigated suburban lawns, still drained the Colorado. Now the Desert Beach golf course painted its dead grass green. Connie turned again, this time down an unnumbered road. Red sand off the basalt mountains drifted across the faded yellow lines.

....

Dennison Smith's first novel, *Scavenger*, was published with Insomniac Press, Toronto. Her second novel, *Eye of the Day*, is appearing with Harper Collins Canada. She is the recipient of Canada Council and Ontario Arts Council grants, Agnes Nixon Award for Playwriting, Francis Lerner Award for Performance Literature, and Stand International Short Story Award.

by Dennison Smith

Siobhan Tumelty

Another Life
Novel Extract

The following is an extract from the first chapter of my novel Another Life.

Across the lane from Michael is a middle-aged woman hovering in a gutter. Her knickers are bunched around her podgy, pastry-dough knees and she's releasing a steaming stream of piss that Seabiscuit would be proud of. It splashes her calves and runs downhill, soaking her satin handbag. She shakes herself a little, loses her balance and falls backwards, flat on her back with her fanny in the air, fat legs flailing hopelessly. As she lies on the pavement shrieking with laughter, her friends – decked in feather boas and pink cowgirl hats – drag the pissy mess to her feet.

'Bit breezy tonight, is it love?' Michael nods at her underwear, half-mast. 'You wanna watch where you're flashing that.'

The woman gives him a sovereign-ringed middle finger, and one of her entourage throws a pork rissole in his direction.

Michael walks away, past Kiwis – home of the MILF – and along Chippy Lane, where the middle-aged punters have gathered for a late night cone. He buys some himself and leans back against a wall, watching the hordes make a last-ditch effort to get their leg over. It's slim pickings. A hefty-looking woman with her shoes dangling from her fingers is trying to convince some bloke to give her a piggyback. He allows himself to be mounted and the top-heavy pair tilt and teeter along the lane like a unicyclist at the circus. Not worth it, Michael thinks, his back will be fucked even if she would be one of the grateful ones. He leaves them to it. The clubs are pulsing. From the pavement, he can hear the bass reverberate – the night-time's thudding heartbeat.

In an hour or so, valley commandos, teenage tarts, rugby heads and nine-to-fivers will spill out onto St Mary's for extra time. It's Michael's favourite part of the evening, all sorts of people from all of the different clubs seeking each other out, congregating for an after-party on the street. Potluck, 10p mixed bag, you never know who you'll bump into. It reminds him of the playground in school – a brief escape where indoor rules don't apply – but for now he enjoys feeling like the whole place is his.

He wanders along the main street, admiring his surroundings, neon club signs, flashing sirens. The street's pedestrianised for Saturday nights, and police hover at both ends. There's one posing for photos with a hen party, bride-to-be looking good in his helmet. Walking past dead-end lanes, Michael can see a girl in the shadows with her skirt hitched up, bracing herself against a wheelie bin. He stops to watch for a moment, and the man pounding away behind her turns to look at him. Michael expects abuse, but the man just grins and gives him the thumbs up. Michael laughs and moves on. He's seen it all before, doled it out himself to women bending over the same walls their mothers did back in 1986. There was beauty in it somewhere, the circle of life – futile twisted comedy like a dog chasing its tail.

He did all right on the bird front. Tall and broad from lumping breeze blocks, he wouldn't call himself handsome, but he had something. Persistent, presumptuous, never afraid to be shot down. Women liked his freckles, his rough labourer's hands. Girls were all right for a night or two but he never let it go on much longer. Too expensive, too demanding of your time. He preferred spending his dole on Jagerbombs and Bow and Black, the cash-in-hand he could get on the side he spent on crisp polo T-shirts and box-fresh trainers.

He heads back to the club where he left his mates, picking through his chips for the crispy ones. He fishes them out and licks salty grease from his fingers, the vinegar stinging his nose. He crumples the paper cone and tosses his left-overs to the floor, just outside the club where he'd left his mates. This catches the doorman's attention.

by Siobhan Tumelty

'What d'you think you're doin there en butt? Thas literrin that is. You're not comin in yur til you pick up every last one of em chips.'

The doorman looks Michael in the eye, crumples up his own cardboard coffee cup and throws it down amongst the piles of crap on the pavement. He sounds like he's come down from Ponty; just a few miles further along the Taff but a world away from Cardiff. His voice is sing-song, and lacks Michael's harsh vowels. On the front of his black woollen coat Michael sees a laminated SIA badge, like a sheriff's star. Gives him carte blanche to do whatever the fuck he pleases. Michael sniggers and tries to walk past him into the club, but the doorman blocks his entrance.

'Where d'you think you're goin? I said pick up em chips!'

There are two women just behind the doorman, bandy-legged and mini-skirted, they're hanging on his every word. One's worth a squirt but the other is rough by anyone's standards. The doorman obviously fancies his chances.

'You having a laugh mate?' Michael says, gesturing at the floor. 'Look at the state of the fuckin place!' He's got to be kidding, playing the joker for the ladies.

The doorman bristles at this – a tomcat with his fur standing on end.

'Who d'you think you're talkin to like that en?' he says. 'Step away from the queue pal, you're not comin in yur.' He straightens himself up to his full five feet ten, but Michael can still see over the top of his head.

'Don't start,' says Michael. 'My mates are in there. I only went out for some chips an some air. You musta seen me, five minutes ago.'

The doorman moves forward and squares his shoulders. He's stocky, with a second row type frame. 'If I tells you to go, en it's time to go.'

Michael swears quietly. He's got his best new T-shirt on, a baby pink polo. His last black eye has only just faded. He weighs up his options.

'Fuck you then mate,' he says, and holds up his hands.

Before Michael can turn away, the doorman charges. He shoves

Michael, luminous yellow credentials flashing on the doorman's arm. The girls stagger out of the way while Michael stumbles back a few paces into the street. He smirks, shaking his head. The doorman pushes him again. Only a twat would let him get away with that, so Michael pulls back a fist and splits his knuckles on the doorman's teeth.

Bending in the middle, the doorman raises a hand to his mouth. He touches his lip, inspects the leather glove glinting patent black with his blood in the light from the street lamp. Michael's hand hurts; he stretches it out, shaking it, testing the fingers. He's got a decent right hook, useful for ending fights rather than prolonging them. Aware of his size, he's always been told to be careful how he uses it.

The doorman looks at the girls to his side. They're far enough away not to get hurt, but close enough for a good view of his defeat. Michael's seen it before: Discovery Channel, David Attenborough, stags with antlers locked. He stands still, waiting, pondering the safety of turning his back on the other man. He breathes heavily and fumbles in his pocket for his asthma inhaler. His body decides for him – fight or flight – and he swivels on his heels. As he does, the doorman takes three quick strides towards him and pushes him hard from behind. He flies forward into an overflowing bin. It crashes to the ground and Michael lurches with it, reaching out to break his fall. He lands with his face inches from a partially digested kebab. Struggling to right himself, he gulps lung-fulls of the vomit reek and flinches at the burning grazed skin of his hands. The pavement's wet, and broken glass winks at him from the gutter. Whilst he's still on all fours, the doorman kicks him with steel toe-capped boots, and drags him to his feet by his T-shirt. It rips. It was sixty quid. A week's dole. Twenty pints. A fucking waste.

Michael wriggles free and catches the doorman in a bear hug, reaching around him, punching his kidneys, but the impact's softened by the bloody big coat. The doorman sinks his teeth into Michael's shoulder, tears skin, drawing blood. Michael lets go, pushing him away.

by Siobhan Tumelty

A crowd has formed around them but no one tries to intervene. The doorman rushes forward with his hands outstretched, reaching for Michael's throat. He pins Michael against the wall and hits him in the face. Michael brings up a knee to the doorman's stomach, winds him, and he drops back. The doorman bends over, looking up at Michael like a taunted bull, gathering his strength. Michael has had enough. He swings a carefully aimed uppercut at the hunched-up doorman, catching him just beneath his jaw. The doorman's head jerks back quickly, grotesquely, and he falls to the ground, spun by the force of the punch. His head hits the pavement and he doesn't get up. Michael collapses in on himself, puts his hands on his knees and sucks big breaths of wet night air, feeling sweat trickle down behind his ears, tickling his neck. The crowd contracts around the doorman, swallowing him in a morbid tide of curiosity. Like flies around shit the police swarm, attracted by the mass of onlookers – thirty seconds too late to be of any use. Michael finds himself pulled away. He is dragged into a van by enthusiastic young constables armed with batons and gas. They don't use them; he is completely submissive. He thinks how easily things could have been different. In another life, that could have been him – epaulettes, radio and a tidy little salary. Dazed, he tongues a wobbly tooth and tastes blood. He spits on the floor of the van, wipes his mouth with his forearm, and rests his handcuffed wrists on his scuffed wet jeans.

Siobhan Tumelty was born in Cardiff in 1986, and studied English and Creative Writing at UWIC before coming to UEA. She has had short stories published in *Planet Magazine* and *The C Word: An Anthology of Writing from Cardiff,* and is currently working on her first novel.

by Siobhan Tumelty

Fuchsia Wilkins

Dynamo 509

You are about to start reading my latest novel, *Dynamo 509*. You saw the front cover in the bookshop and it appealed to you immediately. The blurb only confirmed that this was the type of book you were looking for, a light read, fast-paced, with a twist at the end that you weren't expecting. An exciting crime thriller, detailing the plight of an ex-army vigilante, as he seeks to find out who murdered his young wife, and why. You recognised my name on the spine. You have seen it in the past, on television, in magazine reviews that were all rather favourable. You remember a recommendation from a friend: *'Read Harold Silva,'* they said, *'his writing's pretty good.'* The accumulation of these details all seemed promising, and so you decided to give the book a go, took it to the till and paid your seven ninety-nine.

Back at home, you settle down into an easy chair and place a cup of coffee onto the table in front of you. Or you have just got into bed and are stretching out after a long day, finding yourself suddenly in the mood for some relaxation. *Dynamo 509* is down by the coffee cup; it's lying beside you, ready on the bedside cabinet.

You experience a kind of rising suspense, instilled by the prospect of a new book. But it is nothing compared to the tension you will find within its pages. With *Dynamo 509*, you are in for a story that keeps you guessing, leaves clues and then dismisses them as decoys; leads you to condemn a character for his conduct then alters your view of him because of some utterly redeemable deed. You will, assuredly, become caught up in the life of the protagonist. You will feel the hurts of his past and join his struggle for a future. You will read avariciously, voraciously, and come the finale you will be left wanting more. The ending will contain a surprise. Just wait.

Ignoring all else, you rearrange the pillows behind your head. You crease open the first page and, eagerly, you start to read.

*

The first page isn't so bad. Has enough intrigue to keep me going. I glance at the clock and push aside the paperwork on my desk, the sheets of shorthand, spiral notebooks, make time for thirty minutes with a book as I take the rest of my lunch break. My mind darts momentarily to the review I could be working on, but it's so mind-numbingly dull I really can't be facing it.

I loosen my tie and read on for a few more pages. First chapter done already. It's pretty quick to get through, but what else was I expecting from pulp fiction? Phil is always passing on these kinds of books to me over lunch, *'Try this one, Nick!'* he beams at me. They're the read 'em once then chuck 'em kind. They're not so bad, though they're hardly Shakespeare. Just like enjoying a trashy movie really, and about the same price as a ticket to the cinema.

The plot … well, it's all right, though pretty standard so far. This is one of those generic thriller slash cri-fi novels, with a romantic thread and a dash of deception. The characters are stereotypical, although that Jameson isn't a bad sort. It sounds like he's been through a lot with that wife of his, but from the sound of the backstory, she probably had it coming to her. He's become emotional, typically, which drives the plot. His grief gives him a motive, blah de blah, makes him mad – so of course he's got to hunt the killer down before he can move on and reclaim a life.

It'll be a good romp, I'm sure, but I can already stab a guess as to how it'll end. Emotional redemption and a newfound love; an offer for a position in a high-class intelligence job? And all this after the death of his most trusted friend and sidekick, naturally.

I'd be willing to bet on it. It's how these stories work.

by Fuchsia Wilkins

*

Placing the open book facedown, you pause to re-boil the kettle; you get out of bed to go for a pee. You have just finished Chapter Four and by this point the tension is mounting. The story has you hooked and you hurry with what it is you're doing so that you can make a start on Chapter Five.

By now I have introduced you to most of the main characters. You understand Jameson's reasons for seeking revenge, and feel sympathy towards him; his wife was a sweet girl and her untimely death was far from deserved. *If you'll take the time to read again, you'll find she wasn't the tyrant you mistook her for.* You are grateful to Etney for standing beside Jameson, though you remain wary of the silent silhouette cast over events by the Colonel, despite a growing belief that he may be useful later on. The plot is coming together and you can tell you are in for a whirlwind of adventure. Already you can see that Nadine is not the girl for Jameson, that she will not successfully fill his first wife's shoes. Her allure is clearly cheap and you are willing him to step away.

From a reliable source you have heard there will be a car chase, and somehow you feel this may be coming soon. The kettle boils; hastily, you pull the chain.

You must slow down though, read properly, and take the time to pay attention to detail. *Dynamo 509* has been carefully compounded. You are in danger of taking it purely at face value.

Coffee refilled, bladder satiated, you resume your former position now. You cross your fingers for the car chase, but I'll keep you waiting a little longer. Chapter Five introduces a new mystery. You should be filled with suspense. That was my plan, at least.

*

Despite the obvious narrative this is catching my imagination. I leave the canteen early now, to get my nose stuck in. Amongst the books I have to get through for the week's reviews, this one is light relief. It's compulsive reading matter that's drawn me in, like a bad soap on the telly.

The plot thickens, and Jameson's off to meet someone shady. The date is set in a typically out-of-the-way location, an abandoned electrical plant in the city's outskirt. Beside old generator, '509'. Cliché, or what? That's the room number, too, that his wife was murdered in.

So I can see it already – it'll be an old army buddy with a debt to repay to him, or a relative from his past, a brother or a cousin – someone with useful information about what's going on here. They'll be able to tell Jameson who's sending the letters, or help him to change address. Something like that. This Harold Silva probably thinks he's being original, but as far as I can tell, it's always the same in these pulperback novels.

Jameson is feeling apprehensive. As I make a start on my afternoon work I look over my shoulder, to make sure I know who is behind me. I find myself wondering about blackmail, not book reviews. Double crossings seem more important than deadlines.

I come out of the office at the end of the day and, still in role, I look forward to driving back to my lovely Nadine. I keep an eye out to make sure no one is trailing me – *cue car chase?* – and I check the wing mirrors repeatedly to make sure my lapels are neat, like his.

*

Second coffee finished, and you're up to Chapter Nine. Although at this point you should be shocked, not smug.

How did you deduce that Jameson's contact would be his own brother? I thought I'd set it up so carefully, given the impression that he'd died already, years before. His presence at the generator should have been unexpected, but you spoilt that drama with your second-guessing.

I have no idea, either, why you insist on dressing Jameson like that. Where did 'lapels' come from? A description in the first chapter clearly elucidated his attire: *'He dressed easily, automatically, pulling*

by Fuchsia Wilkins

on his worn leathers, faithful companions that had accompanied him on many a daring excursion in the past.' You were to think of him as rugged, world-worn; but instead you chose to pick up on 'sleek' and 'well-dressed' later on, and your mind jumped immediately to 'suit'.

That is not what Jameson looks like. You should be reading properly. This is my story, after all, not yours to mess around with as you please!

*

I don't like the direction this is taking. Silva is clearly marking out Jameson's brother as the bad guy, but it'd be too obvious. It would be more effective if someone like Etney had done it. He'd be perfect – the silent type, though not dead chilling like they usually are. And he's been too involved in everything up until now even to be considered suspect. It'd be a really clever twist if he turned out to be the murderer.

If it does turn out to be the brother, then, I'm sorry, Harold Silva, but your book will join the chuck 'em pile for sure. Phil can have his book back and I'll move obligingly on to his latest find.

If I was you, I'd invent a grudge for Etney. Something personal against Jameson that he's kept simmering for years, waiting for the right opportunity to strike out and avenge. Maybe a lust for Jameson's wife whilst she was alive, an unrequited love that made him blister? Or perhaps he heard that Jameson tasted his girlfriend once, and all this time he'd pretended not to know.

I'm deviating from the plot that's offered me. Inventing all the twists I'd like to see instead. I see it like a movie reel, and I'm the director, choosing what to cut and change.

Maybe I ought to quit my day job. Take up writing books instead of columns.

*

This is becoming more than a joke.

You were never supposed to guess the brother's part in this! And as for framing Etney is his stead, well ... it's just not on! What the hell do you think you're doing, taking such liberties? You can't just change my plot and disregard my plans. I wrote Etney as a genuine, dependable character; there are never enough of them in this genre. Jameson's brother is the one with the dubious past, with the grudge and the tainted psyche.

If you're going to persist in this line, you may as well cross my name off the cover. You've invented a new book, all of your own, with not a care to the work that I've put in.

You're strangling my narrative, or don't you realise? It seems that you'd make a rather good murderer yourself.

*

BookSpeak
Dynamo 509 by Harold Silva
Review by Nick Beeston

Don't let yourself be put off by the unimpressive cover of *Dynamo 509*, the final literary offering from the late Harold Silva. This is not your average dose of pulp fiction.

The protagonist is an atypical hero of the genre – the well-dressed Jon Jameson, ex-army, just back from the war in Afghanistan.

Wounded by his cheating wife, but wracked by a sense of duty after her sudden murder, Jameson turns vigilante, and, kept in company by his trusted friend Etney, he takes it on himself to hunt and reprimand her killer.

Silva has managed to defy my expectations of sensationalist crime fiction in *Dynamo 509*. He has created striking characters, who never act in the way you anticipate. He constantly keeps you guessing, never falls too far into cliché, and expertly manages to maintain a fast-paced plot.

There have been rumours that Silva originally planned to include a different 'whodunnit' from the one whom appears as culprit in the

by Fuchsia Wilkins

finished book. In my mind the alteration creates a much stronger and highly unexpected ending. It both increases the level of drama and makes for a nail-biting romp, whilst at the same time deviating from the expected conventions of this generally over-subscribed genre.

It was with much sadness, recently, that we learnt of the death of this novelist. I, for one, eagerly await the author who will fill his shoes.

Fuchsia Wilkins gained her undergraduate degree from UEA in 2010. She now divides her time between writing short stories and dancing Argentine tango.

by Fuchsia Wilkins

Life Writing

Introduction
by Kathryn Hughes

Judith Chriqui
Judy O'Kane
Stephen Skelton
Adrian Ward

'Life Writing' has always been a generous tent under which to shelter all manner of literary work. This year our MA students have taken full advantage of that permissive spirit, producing pieces that are, variously, meditative, lyrical and crisply turned.

Stephen Skelton presents us with a piece about his great uncle Eric Gill. Gill was a controversial genius whose private life was not quite as private as perhaps it should have been (there are 130 loving sketches of his own genitalia now housed in the British Museum). Stephen, though, wants us to take a closer look at Gill Sans, that classic typeface that became the badge of mid-century Britain.

Judith Chriqui, meanwhile, heads to Morocco where she and her all-American siblings are obliged to watch mulishly as her father whips himself up into a frenzied search for his ancestors' graves. Adrian Ward jumps between time and cultures in an intricate meditation on the nature of falling (watch out for some particularly spiffy bedroom curtains). Finally Judy O'Kane heads to the south coast of Ireland where she has enrolled on the famous cookery course at Ballymaloe and finds herself obliged to get to grips with a particularly slippery monkfish. Lucky, then, that she's as good a writer as she is a chef.

....

K.H.
Director, MA in Life Writing

by Kathryn Hughes

Judith Chriqui

The Life Cycle of a Frog

The following piece is an excerpt from a short story about my family's trip to Morocco, my father's birthplace.

Essaouira, Morocco

My father holds a piece of paper so tightly it shakes. He is standing over his great grandfather's grave. 'David Derhy Bar Zohora was buried here,' he says, 'around 1940. He was fifty years old when he passed away. Your uncle David is named after him.'

The last Jews left Essaouira in 1967. All that remains now is this cemetery; Jewish only through the faint chisel of Hebrew on the gravestones. I think about the people who lived here, and the stories my father used to tell me about Savta, 'grandmother'.

How she walked through the spice market in her heels to buy butter, how she read love letters from Saba, grandfather, on the synagogue roof, which had the best view of the ocean, how she'd listened to the lively chatter of the Rabbi's daughters every Friday as they stood around the communal ovens in the summer heat, waiting for the Sabbath tagine to bubble. This was her city.

All of that is gone. All of that is gone and we are left with this: an unkempt, lifeless backyard, crammed with eroded lumps of rock. To think my father was born here, in this city; I cannot imagine it. I see him napping peacefully with his brothers and sisters in an oven like little challah breads. Rising. Never born.

'It's the father of Savta Simcha Simi Chriqui of blessed memory,' my father continues.

'Anything anybody wants to say?' None of us wants to say anything. 'Just going to do my ceremony, do a little Tehillim for him, for his soul, and we'll go', he says. He chokes. I think he is crying.

Praise the Lord! Praise the Lord, O my soul. I will sing to the Lord with my soul; I will chant praises to my God while I yet exist.

Mother holds the camera, filming; Joey, my little brother, is turned away from my father, standing in a far corner of the cemetery. My older brother Ariel looks off in another direction. I am beside him, grinding my teeth.

A guard walks in; stares at my father and retreats. We are the only ones here. My mother holds the camera. Dad recites the psalms. He stumbles over the words.

He heals the broken-hearted, and bandages their wounds. He counts the number of the stars; He gives a name to each of them. Great is our Master and abounding in might; His understanding is beyond reckoning.

Ariel spots a frog and follows it around with a feigned curiosity. I resent him for this; he isn't playing along like the rest of us, he isn't even pretending to care. But eventually we all begin watching it too. The frog is bright, and we can see it beating, lime-green and swollen. I think about squeezing it hard, or stepping on it, I want to push the life out of it. Ariel picks it up. My father finishes and turns to us. More of his kin are here, somewhere.

'Judith and Joey, you take cousin Salam. Ariel, you take great grandmother Rachel.'

For over an hour, we make a great effort to be in motion. We hurl our bodies around the cemetery looking for them. We hunt with a sudden, unaccountable determination, until thirty minutes pass and we haven't found anyone. Then finally Joey does spot a name, and my dad pipes up with an animation that feels almost inappropriate. 'We found someone,' he beams at the camera. 'We found someone.'

When his spirit departs, he returns to his earth; on that very day, his plans come to naught. I will exalt You, my God the King, and bless Your Name forever.

Ariel stretches out his palm, letting the frog spring off onto one of the headstones. My father doesn't notice.

....

Judith Chriqui received a BA in English and Creative Writing from Sarah Lawrence College in 2009. Her last major work appeared in *Strangers in Paris*, an anthology of stories and poems about Paris published by Tightrope Books. She currently lives in England.

by Judith Chriqui

Judy O'Kane

The Rocket House

It had been the Coastguard's house. When a boat was in trouble he would send up a flare. It's still there, at the edge of the cliff, at the far end of the village. You could easily miss it: if you look up from the water it's the house with the mustard yellow walls. I stayed there for three months, a stowaway.

The Rocket House was practically suspended over the water. A half door led through to the kitchen, with flagstone tiles and an old-fashioned dresser, crowded with jugs, butter paddles and a torch. The bay window had blue gingham seats and the best view in Ballycotton. That part of the village was an amphitheatre; the houses on the hillside looked down at *Cleopatra, Eagle II, Sarah Marie*, and *Molly Daniel*. Pale blue fishing nets lay tangled beside lobster pots along the pier; the water was so close you could almost reach out and touch it.

*

I unfolded my uniform, white jacket and checked trousers, with nametags sewn into the lining. I was following a well-worn path: for twenty-five years trainee chefs from all over the world had invaded the village, tumbling out of the pubs, flashes of whites flying up the Main Street on bicycles. A few months earlier, before handing over to my locum, I'd taken photographs of the view from my office window: the National Concert Hall, and across St Stephen's Green to the Shelbourne Hotel. The Rocket House had the feel of a medieval hostel, a halfway house.

Sixty of us introduced ourselves on the first day of term. We each said a few words about what had brought us, and whether we intended to pursue a career in food. There were gap year students and lawyers, medics and teachers on career breaks. There was an astrophysics graduate, a nanny, a news anchor, a butcher, a baker and an Olympic rower; one student had just returned from making pies in Russia, another had been guerilla gardening in the States. Some had worked in sustainability and others had cooked in kitchens across London. One girl had sold her radiators to fund the course. When I stood up, I was shocked to see I was shaking. I hadn't realised how much it meant to me. What was I doing here?

We learned about the importance of soil, and composting. We fed kitchen waste to the chickens and kept citrus fruit skin to make candy peel. There were bins in every colour; we were warned not to confuse them. I was terrified of destroying the ecosystem, jeopardising the farm's organic status, so I drove around for weeks with a boot full of rotting rubbish. When it started to ferment, I got rid of the bags.

As the fishermen loaded their boats to go out in the mornings, I raced around for my keys, until I discovered I was the only one for miles to lock my door. I made it in just in time for roll-call, and added to the sound of pots clamouring, jokes and banter, while teachers yelled instructions above the din. In the evenings I retreated to the solitude.

The neighbours would drop in at all hours. Nora invited me into her cottage for a drink. 'What do you do above in Dublin?' she said. 'Would you like a bit of salmon for your tea?' asked Joan, from next door. She called back later. 'It's all arranged,' she said, her musical intonation making every sentence a question. 'You're invited for coffee, a lovely girl just up the road, she's on her own too?'

Men stood at the end of the pier in the evening, their fishing rods pointing out to sea. The odd word floated up, in a Cork lilt, or one of the Slavic languages, but mostly they stood taciturn for hours. Gulls yelled, swallows would dive and swoop. I watched the fishermen unrolling ropes and nets from behind the safety of the

by Judy O'Kane

glass. One night in midsummer a dolphin swam past with her young, performing for the boatload of screaming children following close behind her.

I would fall asleep to the sound of the engines shutting down and drifting into the harbour. One night I wandered over to the window; a boat was gliding in. The water looked like molten chocolate, the V in its wake like someone had run a knife slowly across the surface.

I would wake in the early hours when a beam of light shone across the bed, as dramatic as the monolithic chamber in Newgrange at winter solstice.

The fishermen went out in all weathers, in jeans and T-shirts, or wax overalls when it was rough; they didn't wear sunglasses and they had never learned to swim. At night their engines were the only sounds. I imagined they were police boats chugging up the canals in Venice, or Mafioso pulling onto the lake outside Michael Corleone's house to take some poor soul to sleep with the fishes.

The harbour was sheltered by two piers, which almost touched. The water was so clear you could see the purple jellyfish. Boys jumped off in midsummer, without wetsuits, hitting the water with a crash. The place was alive with flashes of bright yellow galoshes; friends chatted as they passed my door with fishing gear, and excited children pulled on their life jackets. Dogs stood on the side of the road, watching the traffic go past. The headlines on the newspaper stand read, NEW SEASON BRITISH QUEENS.

On hot days the sky would go from pale to dark blue, then pink, purple, and sometimes orange, the colours of a bruise healing. When it was wet, it took on a grey light; rain punctured the water, leaving tiny concentric circles and afterwards, crystal beads hung from cobwebs. I wanted to capture it all. I took photographs of the harbour reflected in a raindrop, the boats out of focus, our textbook in the foreground, *Ballymaloe Cookery Course*.

*

After class, we gathered wild garlic for pesto and swung from branches, grabbing elderflower to make cordial. We hung around the greenhouses inspecting our seedlings. The car was covered in sand, towels dried out on the back window. On weekends we would meet up at the Farmers' Market in Midleton. We tasted smoked salmon, chorizo and cheeses from West Cork, and carried home bags of baby beetroots and carrots, the fronds hanging out over the tops of the bags. I bought cherry tomatoes, and left them in the oven overnight, till they shrivelled and turned up at the edges like little saucers. We walked down to the pier, carrying mugs of tea, so we wouldn't look like tourists. We wanted to buy something from the catch; we were directed to Declan. 'What size do you want, large or handy?' he asked. He gave us a massive cod and wouldn't take anything for it. When we told the barman in the Blackbird later that evening, he said, 'sure, won't it bring luck to the boat?'

It took me a while to come to terms with killing anything myself. I just managed to get the Pyrex lid on over the lobsters while they changed colour. I sat outside and read how to kill a lobster humanely. You could put it into tepid water, and let it fall sleep as the temperature increased, or drop it straight into boiling water, or alternatively you could plunge a knife between its eyes. I wondered if the chefs believed their own propaganda and grabbed the glass out of Nora's hand as soon as she invited me over.

Ten of us went out on Peter's fishing boat, followed by hordes of birds. I squirmed as the mackerel wriggled on the line. 'Is it dead?' I asked. 'Hold on till I ask him,' Peter said. 'He says he's dead.' We took knives to them quickly, pushed the blade up along the spine on both sides and threw what was left to the gulls. We chopped, swaying with the waves as the birds squawked and raced for the scraps, while Peggy and Melody lay groaning with their feet up the side of the boat. We stank of sweat and bird droppings, our bloody hands smeared across cameras to record each other holding up the fish. The GPS on my camera had logged my co-ordinates: Ballycotton, County Cork. I belonged here.

The lifeboat, Austin Linbury, sat in between the boats. It

by Judy O'Kane

spluttered out purple fumes every week as volunteers ran up and down the decks, but sometimes they weren't drills, and I would listen to the rescue chopper all night. The next day I would dread turning on the radio.

On Sunday nights the trawlers would come into the harbour, dwarfing the rest of the boats. The crew loaded fish into articulated trucks, which pulled away in the early hours, their gears straining on the hill. The fishermen were good-natured, relieved to have company after eight days at sea. They drank whiskey at Lynch's; they said very little and turned their heads every time the door opened.

Michael, the taxi driver and part-time fisherman, asked me what I was cooking for the exam. He left in a monkfish to practise and wouldn't hear of payment. 'Ah, I wouldn't charge you for just the one.' It was enormous; it almost filled the fish crate. It had a slimy film and slipped across the chopping board.

I pulled leaves off the herbs we would be tested on, and Sellotaped them onto my notes. We were encouraged to take home cuttings; they sat on the windowsill, attracting fruit flies. I borrowed books from the library and sat spellbound by Steiner's system of biodynamics, where the moon charts optimal days for planting, harvesting and tasting. While I read about pinot noir production in New Zealand, the soil in the pots dried out, the leaves and stalks became desiccated bundles for the recycling bin.

I imagined that I dissolved into the landscape, but to others I was the stranger, the outsider, the other. The week I moved in, before I had met a sinner, there was a loud knock at the door. I opened to see a Guard and behind him, Fred, who had driven down from Dublin. 'This man here was lookin' for you,' he said, stepping back to make sure he hadn't led a violent criminal to my door.

We went across the road to Nautilus. We were the only ones in the restaurant and had to keep lowering our voices. When the food arrived Fred said, 'You're looking at that through new eyes.'

*

I handle the photos now like a forensic scientist. I have them backed up onto hard disks and saved online. I have them printed out and pinned up around my study like exhibits from a crime scene. They are fragile, irreplaceable: evidence of another life. I see myself in front of the bay window, smiling into the camera, dismembered crabs lying across the chopping board, beside the hammer we used to break the shells.

'What has you down here anyway?' the fisherman had asked the day he took me out to haul lobster pots.

I knew I couldn't stay and that when I returned I would be a visitor. 'You won't fit back in the way you did before you left,' a consultant had told me years before, while I was on secondment. 'It's like taking a letter out of an envelope: it doesn't go back in the way it came out.'

The morning I left, before I finally took off, past the fuchsia hanging down over the dry-stone walls, I fastened the bike onto the back of the car. Joan appeared, 'You loved it here,' she said. 'You're welcome to come back and stay any time. It'd be no trouble. No trouble at all.'

....

Judy O'Kane was shortlisted at Listowel Writers Week in 2012 in the humorous essay category and was a winner of Tremors Short Story Competition. Her work has appeared in *Fire & Knives*. She is writing a creative non-fiction account of cookery classes from Ireland to India. Judy is a solicitor in Dublin.

by Judy O'Kane

Stephen Skelton

Gill Sans

Arthur Eric Rowton Gill (1882–1940) was a supremely talented – yet controversial – artist. His achievements, the Stations of the Cross in Westminster Cathedral, the statue of Prospero and Ariel over the front door to Broadcasting House and his typeface, Gill Sans, to name but three of his most enduring, are there for all to see. But his failings as a human being are also well known. His unconventional views on religion, the wearing of trousers (he preferred a loose, belted smock), underwear (he typically wore none) and man's 'most treasured possession' (there are 130 exquisite drawings of his own genitalia in the British Museum) set him firmly apart from the crowd. To these though, must be added the incest he committed with his own daughters and at least one of his sisters (my grandmother Angela) – and his 'experiments' with his dog (today we would call it nothing more than bestiality) – all of which he recorded in his diaries and which he knew would eventually see the light of day. Whether Gill should be admired for his talents or ostracised for his failings, there is no doubt that his sans serif typeface remains his most widely seen achievement.

(This essay, except where examples of other typefaces are used, is set in Joanna, a typeface Gill designed in 1930-31.)

In October 1926 Gill took his family to live in Wales in a small hamlet called Capel-y-ffin, near Abergavenny, and was invited by a friend, Douglas Cleverdon, to paint a fascia board for the bookshop Cleverdon was opening in Bristol. On arriving there, Gill developed 'a slight attack of influenza' and had to retire to bed. Thinking that Gill might be bored, Cleverdon took him a blank sketching book for him to draw 'a couple of alphabets, in roman and sans serif, which I could use as models for notices in the bookshop'. After a day in bed, Gill got up and made a start on the fascia and after a morning working on it, stopped to go to a matinée at the theatre, returning to draw the alphabets that evening. The fascia he finished the next day. Five months later, Stanley Morison, a friend of Cleverdon's and an admirer of Gill's work, came to stay for the weekend. Morison, who had already commissioned Gill to produce a serif typeface which would

be released as Perpetua in 1929[1], was greatly impressed by both the shop front, the alphabets and a metal name-plate which simply said:

....

1	Perpetua, with its original punches hand-cut by the great French punch cutter, Charles Malin, became one of Monotype's most successful typefaces and after Times New Roman and Gill Sans, its third most widely sold font. Monotype Recorder, 1958, p.10.

by Stephen Skelton

CLEVERDON [2].

Morison, a largely self-taught typographer, was the 'Typographical Advisor' to the Monotype Corporation who were developing the most advanced form of typecasting machine that the printing world had then seen. The Super Caster, released in 1928, could house a wide variation of fonts which could be expanded to 72 point size in a large number of different formats. Monotype also allowed printers to hire matrices for the Super Caster, an innovation in the printing world[3]. It was, in all senses of the word, a super typecaster and needed a new super-type, especially one adapted to the requirements of the display and advertising printing community, who valued modernity over tradition. Morison decided it needed a modern sans serif typeface and that Gill was the man for the job. In June 1927, the forty-three-year-old Gill started work on the designs, which Morison (to Gill's amusement) said ought to be known as 'Gill Sans'.

Although it may have been the shop front that Morison admired and which prompted him to commission Gill Sans, Gill had already been experimenting with a bold, block-letter type. Gill had used 'free sans serif lettering more or less derived from the type designed for the London Underground Railways by Edward Johnston'[4] for painting directional signs – 'This way to the Church' etc. – in and around Capel-y-ffin (and it was probably these that Cleverdon saw and liked and wanted for his shop fascia)[5].

Johnston, whose classes in 'calligraphy and illumination' Gill had attended in 1899-1902, was a close personal friend of Gill's, had lived

....

2	Monotype Recorder, 1958, p.15.
3	Personal communication with James Mosley, 12 March 2012.
4	Gill, *Autobiography*, 1941, p.229.
5	Monotype Recorder, 1958, p.14.

in the same Sussex village of Ditchling as Gill and had employed him in the early stages of the development of his Underground typeface. Exactly how much Gill Sans owes to Johnston Underground is still a much-debated topic in the world of typography.

Gill was taken on by Monotype on a salary and the first part of the commission was to produce a set of 'titling capitals' which were first shown at the Annual Meeting of the Federation of Master Printers held in Blackpool in May 1928. Morison gave a talk entitled 'Robbing the Printer' in which he warned printers that if they didn't watch out, some of their work would be taken by advertising and publicity agents who were very much more in tune with modern trends in design and display. Gill's lettering had been used by Morison to title a programme cover for part of the annual meeting. The cover stated:

PUBLICITY AND SELLING CONGRESS

in a somewhat bold, startling way, guaranteed to get the printers off their seats. On being asked whether the programme was 'beautiful' Morison said he couldn't say what was beautiful, but said 'I think my programme had its uses. I saw Mr Hazell kill a fly with his copy'[6] (Hazell was a leading printer of the day). Gill's designs did not meet with universal approval and Morison said that 'an insolent and truculent section' of the Master Printers had described them as 'typographical bolshevism'[7].

Many printers thought that fashion should play no part in typefaces and that there were already plenty available. Manufacturers of typecasting machines however, thought otherwise and knew that if they could create a demand from book designers and publishers for 'modern' typefaces (especially if they had a hand in producing them and – of course – owned the rights to them) then nothing but good could come of it. Monotype employed its own type designers and much of the development work of Gill Sans was done to Gill's original

6 Moran, 1971, p.118.
7 Cleverdon, 1987, p.10.

drawings or based upon guidelines that he drew up. Gill often visited Monotype's London offices in Fetter Lane, just off Fleet Street in the heart of the newspaper printing area, and the sight of him striding up the street, dressed in his trademark beret, belted smock and knee length thick knitted socks, was much prized.

a b c b d e f g h i j k l m n o p q r s t u v w x y z

London and North Eastern Railway

The first major breakthrough for Gill Sans came in 1929 with the decision by the L.N.E.R. to unify all printed material, advertising, station signage and – much to Gill's pleasure (having been a train enthusiast since he was a young boy) – their locomotives and rolling stock. The L.N.E.R.'s advertising manager was William Teasdale who was much influenced by Frank Pick, London Underground's publicity manager, and followed a similar path with publicity material. Teasdale's assistant, C. C. G. (Cecil) Dandridge, who took over when Teasdale was promoted, decided that Gill Sans would suit their purposes very well. Some ninety printers – who between them printed 40 million handbills, leaflets, timetables and pamphlets a year[8] – had to install Gill Sans. The adoption by the L.N.E.R. also afforded Gill one of his proudest, if least likely, moments of pleasure. In 1932, with all the lettering changed, Dandridge decided that there had to be what today we would call a 'photo opportunity' and got Gill to pose besides their best-known service, the Flying Scotsman. The sign on the front of the train had actually been hand-painted and affixed by Gill, for which pains he achieved a lifelong ambition – a ride on the footplate. He travelled from King's Cross to Grantham and wrote an account of it for the *London and North Eastern Railway Magazine*[9]. By 1935, the typeface was 'the largest related series of types for modern composition

....

8   'L.N.E.R. Standardization', Monotype Recorder No. 32, Winter 1932.
9   MacCarthy, 1989, p251.

and display ever based on a single design'[10]. Gill Sans remained the L.N.E.R.'s standard typeface until 1948, when Britain's railways were nationalised, and then Gill Sans was used throughout the whole of British Rail's extensive transport system that encompassed not only trains, but hotels, ferries, buses, and freight haulage companies. Only in the 1960s was a new typeface – New Rail Alphabet – introduced. Vestiges of Gill Sans can still be found hidden around the UK's railway system.

Gill, above, wearing his customary beret and smock beneath his overcoat.

Publishing

One of the first publishers to adopt Gill Sans was The Bodley Head with their new paperback line, Penguin Books. Founded in 1935 and

....

10   Moran, 1971, p 120.

modelled unashamedly on the German imprint Albatross Books which also used a sans serif typeface for their front covers and spine, Penguin's first book, *Ariel* by André Maurois, used Gill Sans and Gill Sans Bold for cover and spine. The designer was a 21-year-old office junior, Edward Young, who was also sent out to sketch a penguin! 'My God how those birds stink' he commented when he returned from London Zoo[11]. Gill Sans survived the period (1947-8) that noted German typographer and book designer Jan Tschichold spent at Penguin. In the 1950s, Penguin's dependence on Gill Sans lessened and although it can still be found on some of today's titles, it is a rarity and Futura is the preferred sans serif typeface.

British Broadcasting Corporation

Despite Eric Gill's association with the BBC – he carved the statue of Prospero and Ariel over the front door to Broadcasting House in 1932-3, as well as a statue called The Sower in the entrance lobby – the choice of Gill Sans for the corporate typeface, used for almost all its printed output as well as its on-screen graphics, its ident and its websites, stems from 1997. Patrick Cramsie, author of *The Story of Graphic Design* felt that the popularity of Gill Sans was because of: '(i) the typeface's inherent qualities, (ii) its extensive range of weights and styles (very light to

....

11   Baines, 2005.

Gill Sans

very bold, etc., which means it can be used in many situations: posters, railway timetables, etc.) and also, importantly, (iii) its familiarity (to British eyes, at least)'. He also stated that its: 'familiarity has bred strong national preferences for particular fonts. Often it stems from a rank, but entirely logical or appropriate, nationalism. I'm sure the BBC, for example, was persuaded to use Gill Sans partly because 'a British institution should use a British typeface'[12].

The Church of England

When the Church of England updated their Common Worship Services and Prayers they selected the designs put forward by Derek Birdsall from his Omnific design studio who wrote: 'It is appropriate to use an English type design and obvious candidates were the types of Eric Gill, namely Joanna, Perpetua and Gill Sans. Trial pages were prepared in these types together with Univers, Bell and News Gothic. As a clear distinction was required between the words spoken by the priest, the congregation, and from the instructions, the ideal typeface would have equally clear distinction between the Roman, bold and italic. Early research and trial proofs showed Gill Sans to be by far the clearest: this is partly because it is designed on humanist lines (particularly the rather cursive italic) and because there is the clearest distinction between Roman, italic and bold; indeed they are distinct but obviously related typefaces.'

....

12   Personal communication with Patrick Cramsie, 20 March 2012.

by Stephen Skelton

Gill Sans, designed 85 years ago, remains one of the world's best known and used typefaces, not only in the printing world, but also on business and home computers. Although based upon a geometric grid, it has a personality and humanity which lift it above other sans serif typefaces.

Bibliography

Baines, Phil
Penguin by Design. A cover story 1935-2005. London, Allen Lane, 2005.

Cleverdon, Douglas
A book of alphabets for Douglas Cleverdon drawn by Eric Gill, Wellingborough, Skelton, 1987.

Gill, Eric
An essay on typography, London, Sheed and Ward, 1936.
Autobiography, New York, Devin-Adair, 1941.

MacCarthy, Fiona
Eric Gill, London, Faber and Faber, 1989.

Monotype Recorder, The. Vol. 36. No. 4.
L.N.E.R Standardization London, author unknown, 1938.

Monotype Recorder, The. Vol. 41. No. 3.
Eric Gill: Master of Lettering, London, author unknown, probably Stanley Morison, 1958.

Moran, James
Stanley Morison, his typographic achievement, London, Lund Humphries, 1971.

....

Stephen Skelton has spent most of his working life growing grapes and making wine in the UK and is a Master of Wine. He has always written, although mainly on wine and viticulture. Now in his mid-sixties, he has decided that an MA in Life Writing will set him on the right path to his next career!

Gill Sans

Adrian Ward

The Cloth

Late in the day at the edge of a small town in India, the breeze pushes a heap of dust along a few paces then waits before moving it on again. In the mottled shade of the jujube trees the cattle shift in the heat, and under her roadside veranda a girl quietly puffs out her cheeks and brushes away a strand of hair from her face with the back of her hand. She spreads a plain cloth over a table, smoothing it out with her palms and placing a flat stone at each corner. She lays pieces of coloured fabric beside each other on the cloth: patches of blue and green, strips of purple and turquoise, a casual collection of shapes and sizes that she arranges loosely together.

She stitches the cloth across and back with coloured threads, then sews a hundred tiny mirrors into place, in what is almost a regular pattern but never completely so. She moves quickly now, and is so familiar with what she does that she hardly needs to look, and can dart her eyes across to where her mother and grandmother sit at their own work; but she also turns occasionally to look out along the road towards the horizon. Behind her a pile of cloths is slowly stacking, ready to be washed and dried. There are little mounds of cloth patches around her, and a semi-circle of open boxes filled with sequins and mirrors, pins and beads, and reels of cotton threads in many shades. The work is repetitive and almost silent except for the girl's humming, which is soft like a lullaby. As she completes her task she lifts the embroidered cloth and shakes it gently over the table for any loose pieces to fall away, then folds it over to stack behind her. She sweeps away the scraps and threads, brushes the hair from her face again, then smoothes out another cloth across the table.

by Adrian Ward

*

On a fog-dimmed morning in Norfolk I draw back one curtain then the other and return to my bed to stare at the embroidered fabric on the wall. Purple and blue, turquoise and green. Irregular patches of cotton and silk, stitched together with twists of thread, dotted around with mirrors – little pools of light and shade. At certain times of day the mirrors seem blank like empty eyes, while in darker moments they are unnervingly deep: either way they require full attention. The coloured cotton patches seem to move together intimately, as if pulling each other into each other, and all merging into something greater but harder to bring into focus. The close colours and similar shapes nudge together into a single cosmology, held in place by broad meandering threads. Sometimes it feels hard to bring my eyes back far enough from gazing into the depths of the cloth and to view it as simply a wall-hanging.

For months I have gazed at this cloth, scanning its surface repeatedly, always hoping to find the patterns or trace the connections and yet never quite seeing them. I can watch for many hours at a time, sometimes completely detached from the passing of the day, having become dazed and disoriented after an accident.

I was on holiday in Italy, and broke my right arm in a heavy fall, damaging the nerve and leaving uncertainty as to whether I will ever be able to move that hand again. It was only a simple fall from a bicycle while going to the shop for bread, but it was serious, and the damage seems out of proportion to the event. The humerus, the large bone in the upper arm, fractured into several pieces, *pluriframmenti* on the doctor's notes, but it is the wrist and the fingers which are not functioning. However many times I replay in my mind the incident and its aftermath it still makes no sense. Nothing really connects. I have been paralysed and traumatised by what was only a moment's misfortune as the rim of the wheel nipped the edge of a kerb and smacked me on to the ground.

*

I can see one window on each side of the room, and the cloth hangs on the wall opposite me. Outside the right-hand window is a large magnolia whose buds sit patiently all through the winter. They swell gradually in February, and finally spread out their display in March, if frost allows. Through the other window, looking east, I can see across the lane to the great tree that stands opposite, a vast and spreading oak whose heavy limbs reach wide. It is like living beside a cathedral: a massive structure which seems lit from inside when the sun rises behind it. On an autumn afternoon the oak catches the full force of the red glow when the sun goes down, and a glorious music seems to rise from within. Every morning squirrels race along the branches as if to bring news, skimming across in an instant from one tip of a twig, through the heart of the tree then out to the farthest reach of an opposite branch – and way beyond, with a hopping leap to the next tree, before disappearing into the greenery.

In the early hours when the cloth is almost completely dark, only the mirrors suggest any sort of presence as they begin to pick out stray beams of light and reflect them back into the room, spots of brightness with no context or connection. But as the rising sun brings more light into the room, filtered through the oak leaves, different mirrors first gleam and then fade, as if in some sloweddown reprise of the pulse of a star, showing and fading, arriving and departing in long cycles.

As the light develops I watch the green and blue shapes merging into and out of each other, the bright glass fragments shifting themselves into groupings of four or five, diamonds and pentagons, these new groups then linking together into wider networks. It feels as if I am looking down from above on a lake-covered landscape in which a thousand small patches of water are laid randomly over the land, some of them surrounded by groups of log cabins or huts. On the cloth there are stitchings in short straight lines which on the

by Adrian Ward

ground might be ridges for cultivation – rice paddies, olive groves, homesteads with food crops to support people in their simplest needs. Broader twists of bright blue threads push their way along the edges of the shapes, like canals or rivers marking out the boundaries. Then there are the longer wider curves of woven thread, barely perceptible, but linking around and beyond these communities as if they are the contours on a map placed over the aerial image – and hinting at other ways in which the disparate might turn out to be connected, perhaps by paths around the hillsides or bridleways down along the bottoms of the valleys.

*

In the background I hear the music of the Malian singer Salif Keita, whose songs of a soft and lilting yearning accompany me through this time. I listen to these insistent songs repeatedly, and while some of them are in French, with lines such as *'Donne-moi ton coeur'* and *'Tu vas me manquer',* most of them are in Bambara, an African language which means nothing to me, but I dissolve my attention into Salif's soaring voice and gently repeated rhythms.

Again I scan and search, this time ranging over the music itself, and while the literal sense of the words is just out of reach, I can still connect to something of their meaning through the sounds of the instruments and the timbre of the voices. *'Tu vas me manquer'* is sung like a litany of lost love as the singer tours across different parts of central Africa – mentioning Ouagadougou, Senegal and its capital Dakar, but always longing for home and family. I hear this as a lament for what is left behind when moving on from one place or one person to another, as well as for something deeper which is always being lost as life moves by, some trace of the self which disappears from view as it soaks away into the sand.

Salif is albino and has suffered the rejection and ridicule which this condition still brings in many parts of Africa. This pain is present in much of his music, which often suggests the feeling of wrapping oneself in the blanket of a rhythmic sound to protect oneself from raw emotion. It is the music of repetition, of trance and the eternal. Sometimes a phrase is repeated twenty or thirty times or more, until whatever language it may have begun in evolves into a flowing river of syllables and intonations, washing away the footprints of any conscious meaning.

So in the act of listening I simply wait for some understanding to arrive, not so much through the words as through their sounds. Years ago when I saw Hugh Masakela perform, a man next to me complained after the first song that because he couldn't understand the words he was not able to enjoy the music, whereas for me the opposite had been true – it was only because I didn't speak Xhosa that I could release myself fully to the immediate experience of the sound.

This scanning to and fro, across and back, as I gaze at this hanging cloth and listen to Salif's voice, is how we read both art and music. It is also how I try to read my own life – travelling back over the gaps and the missing threads, wondering about the spaces and distant views now lost, and holding on tight to the few solid facts to see what might emerge from these. No matter if the first scan produces nothing – just live with it, go back and run it again, pick up the thread and find the tune, listening for a phrase that might offer a connection. If there is still nothing, just allow some other thought to flow across the field of consciousness as if it does hold meaning. Over time and then more time, some meaning will evolve, maybe sometimes with the clarity of a realisation, but mostly arriving in the mind in the way that a returning traveller might enter the town, on

by Adrian Ward

an unseen road and without fanfare – a traveller who pauses for a few minutes in a quiet café on a sidestreet, and only then moves through to the town square to take up his place and spread his cloth across the ochre ground to rest.

....

Adrian Ward is working on a book about the nature and experience of falling, from which this extract is taken. He is interested in psychoanalysis and therapeutic communities, having taught at the Tavistock Clinic in London, and he wrote and edited extensively in that field before taking up life writing and creative non-fiction.

by Adrian Ward